WE CAN DO THIS!

Sacramento's Trailblazing Political Women and the Community They Shaped

Christine Hunter

Library of Congress Control Number 2021919871
ISBN 978-1-952337-47-5
I Street Press
828 I Street, Sacramento, CA 95814
First Edition: January 2022

Cover art by Jasmine Moffett and design by Vanessa Perez
Book layout by Sam Cowan
For information please visit www.wecandothissacramento.com

Dedication

This book is dedicated to Sacramento's trailblazing political women and the community that benefited from their vision, compassion, and perseverance. In loving memory of Frances Gracechild, Virginia Moose, Bonnie Pannell, Lynn Robie, Jean Runyon, Karolyn Simon, and my mother, Joanne Long, who paved the way in the 1950s and 1960s.

Shortly before printing this book news broke that Anne Rudin, the inspiration for many women who followed her lead in 1971, had died. Sacramento's love for her abides and her legacy endures.

Photo courtesy of Christine Hunter Family Collection

"She Did It!" Sacramento League of Women Voters (LWV) president Joanne Long boarding a fighter jet in 1960 - to gain perspective on the region

Profits from the sale of *We Can Do This!*
will be donated to the Sacramento League of Women Voters
Anne Rudin Scholarship Fund

Acknowledgements

The author is deeply grateful to the women who consented to be interviewed and share their personal stories, challenges, and victories as they worked to improve local governance in Sacramento. Research and writing contributions were made by Michele Drier, Heather Fargo, Virginia Kidd, and Mary Ellen Shay. Special thanks to the women who read all or part of the manuscript, providing valuable feedback: Christy Anderson, Heather Fargo, Jane Hagedorn, Lauren Hammond, Lyla Ferris Hanson, Muriel Johnson, Pam Johnson, Joyce Mihanovich, Kim Mueller, Elly Silverman, Susie Swatt, and Susan Willoughby. Proofreading was done by Laurie Hensley and Barbara Rudin. Editing was provided by Nancy Compton, past president of the Sacramento League of Women Voters. The formatting and design of this book was the work of Sam Cowan. Thank you!

Contents

What This Book is About

This book came from a brief discussion several years ago among a group of women who had served as appointed and elected officials in the City and County of Sacramento beginning in the early '70s. With the realization that these women were not only friends, but important trailblazers, research for *We Can Do This!* began.

Thanks to a 1971 change in how city voters elected their representatives to the City Council, opportunities opened up for women to challenge male incumbents and run for public office. Women not only seized the moment to run for local office, but they took a different approach than their well-heeled and well-connected male rivals in how they connected to potential voters. The female candidates campaigned door-to-door to better understand the issues of concern to residents in the diverse neighborhoods of their districts. And once they were elected, female representatives paid close attention to their constituents, responding quickly to the questions, complaints, and suggestions of voters.

In 1971, Anne Rudin took office as City Council representative for District 4, the first woman elected under the new district-based elections. Sacramento County voters had always elected their supervisors by district, and in 1972 Sandra Smoley became the first woman to be elected to the County Board of Supervisors, the only woman competing against seven men.

The time was right for women to represent their communities and they seized the opportunity to serve on appointive bodies and run for local office, helping each other every step of the way. By 1989, five women had won seats on the nine-member City Council and served the people of Sacramento, including Anne Rudin, Lynn Robie

(1980), Lyla Ferris and Kim Mueller (1987), and Heather Fargo (1989). These women represent the first wave of elected women to the Council. (Two additional women were appointed: Callie Carney in 1976 and Eva Garcia in 1983. Carney ran unsuccessfully and Garcia declined to run for Council after completing their appointed terms in office.)

A second wave of women made their mark on the City Council with the election of Deborah Ortiz in 1992, Lauren Hammond in 1997, Bonnie Pannell in 1998, and Sandy Sheedy in 2000. These women served with Sacramento's second popularly elected female Mayor, Heather Fargo (first elected mayor in 2000 and served through 2008). By 2009 there were just three women serving on the Council: Lauren Hammond, Sandy Sheedy, and Bonnie Pannell. In 2010, when Angelique Ashby was elected (re-elected in 2014 and 2018), she was the only woman on the Council. Ten years later, with the election of Katie Valenzuela and Mai Vang in 2020, there were three women on the Council, the third Latina and the first Asian woman elected to the body.

The pace of women being elected to the five-member Sacramento County Board of Supervisors has been more gradual. After Sandra Smoley's election to represent the Third District in 1972, Illa Collin joined her in 1979, representing the Second District, and they were the only two women on the five-member Board. In 1992, Smoley's good friend, Muriel Johnson, replaced her on the Board to represent the Third District, followed by Susan Peters, first elected in 2004. The fifth and sixth women to serve on the board are Roberta MacGlashan (2005-2016) and Sue Frost (2017 to the present).

This book celebrates the achievements of a cross section of the women who have dared to challenge the status quo and who helped make Sacramento the vibrant community it is. While it is not an exhaustive survey of each and every accomplishment of all of Sacramento's elected and noteworthy women, it is intended to highlight and humanize these particular women's contributions for the betterment of society. Each woman brought her own unique perspective to the challenges and opportunities she saw in her community. Some shared a common upbringing during the Depression. Some had the good fortune to be raised in the boom years following World War II. Some had the perspective of being raised in an immigrant or minority community. Most had deep religious or moral convictions that informed their decision making. Every woman applied her intellect, compassion, and vision to the challenges at hand. Let's explore the varied ways Sacramento's trailblazing women proudly declared, "We can do this!"

INTRODUCTION

Nothing is more wholesome for America than the increased participation of women in our government and our politics.
> —Nancy Pelosi, Speaker of the House of Representatives,
> April 23, 2019

Laughter rang out from the corner table of the mostly quiet and subdued Plates Cafe in Sacramento. The quality of laughter was as varied as the women sharing lunch together. A chortle mixed with a giggle that blended with a husky ironic laugh, which in turn released peals of irreverent glee.

This group of women was not just a group of idle oldsters out for a monthly luncheon. They were some of the most influential women in Sacramento's history, women who shaped Sacramento's vision and local government structures from the early 1970s into the early twenty-first century. They included two Sacramento Mayors, four Sacramento City Councilmembers, Chairwoman of the Sacramento County Board of Supervisors, two administrative assistants to a Board member, several leaders of local advocacy groups, as well as dedicated members of local planning commissions, health and human service bodies, and resource-protection boards.

These women broke the "glass ceiling" of local politics well before the term was coined. Who were these women and what did they have in common beyond irreverent glee? Those who ran for elective office did so following the protracted period of all-white-male cronyism that has dominated American politics from the start. They were shut out of Sacramento's all-male Sutter Club, had difficulty raising money, and were initially dismissed as serious contenders by the establishment. What they had from the start was steely determination and the support of friends, family, and neighbors willing to volunteer endless hours licking envelopes, planning fundraisers, and walking door-to-door on their behalf. The secret weapon of these early female activists, at least at the start, was the fact that many of the "old boys" in business and government didn't take them seriously!

While the term "sisterhood" wouldn't necessarily describe this group of women, they were sisters in the finest sense. Each was raised with a strong sense of civic duty, and their contributions to the community often began in local arts, public health, environmental causes, community service, and women's organizations. Many female volunteers attained leadership positions in these civic-minded groups.

When the male power structures of the '70s and '80s stubbornly chose to shut them out, these women invented alternatives such as the Sacramento Women's Network and the Emily Bissell Club (honoring the founder of the Christmas Seals fundraising drive to eradicate tuberculosis).

While many elected and appointed women who challenged the status quo of the '70s, '80s, and '90s are now mostly retired, their protection of the environment and support of Sacramento's social and cultural fabric abides. Their legacy is visible throughout the Sacramento region in the form of a 31-mile parkway along the American River, an urban forest of a million trees, agricultural land preservation, light rail transit lines, new transit-oriented development, urban renewal for residential and commercial use, preservation of historic structures, establishment of community centers and services for long-neglected populations, as well as museums, theaters, and other performing arts centers. Less visible are the policies and procedures these women fostered to make government decision-making processes more open and fair.

Although the attainment and exercise of power and influence by women is in many ways similar to that of men, in other more fundamental ways it is not. This book is an exploration of the development of a unique group of female political leaders, including the influences that gave them the courage to advocate for change and for some to run for elective office. Their goals, insights, and reminiscences described in the following pages are intended to enrich and humanize our understanding of Sacramento's history.

In 2019, public television station KVIE held a discussion of the importance of women's history on the show, *Studio Sacramento*. Diana Madoshi, speaking for the National Women's History Alliance, noted that knowing what women have done before "gives women pride." Former Mayor Heather Fargo added, "And a sense of possibility." The author hopes this book will inspire another generation of Sacramento women to volunteer locally and run for elective office.

Part One

CHAPTER ONE

What Women Faced

In 1971, the city of Sacramento changed the way voters elected City Council members. Rather than choosing among citywide candidates elected at large, voters in each of eight districts would elect their area representative. Because the system was new, all council seats were up for election at the same time, and in late 1971 eight new council members stood ready to assume office. To mark the importance of the occasion, the Chamber of Commerce hosted a reception in their honor at the prestigious Sutter Club, a premier gathering place for city leaders. The reception was to be a welcoming celebration for the incoming council members and an endorsement of the new system.

There was just one problem: the Sutter Club did not admit women, and District 4 had just elected a female, a nurse and political newcomer named Anne Rudin. She was, of course, excluded from the Sutter Club and, thus, the event.

This single example says it all. In 1971, Sacramento—and the larger United States, as well—stood on the brink of a changing culture. Even as voters were beginning to choose female leaders, women were legally still allowed to be treated as inferiors. Change was in the air, but the traditional system did not open its arms wide in a welcoming embrace. In fact, even when by-then Mayor Anne Rudin began her first term in 1984, the Sutter Club still admitted only males. (To their credit, a number of

Photo courtesy of Center for Sacramento History, Online Collection

Mayor Anne Rudin, Sacramento LWV president, 1960-1961, City Councilmember, 1971-1983, and the city's first popularly elected female mayor, 1983-1992

male council members, including future mayor Phil Isenberg, refused to attend Sutter Club events because of the male-only policy.)

When a city's elected leaders can be turned away because of gender, it doesn't take much effort to imagine how other women are treated. Nonetheless, multiple women who faced such constraints emerged in the next few decades to run for office, win, and provide the leadership and wisdom needed to lead the city. Anne Rudin and Sandra Smoley were just the first wave in a sea of active, strong women who would move into important roles in Sacramento city and county governance in the coming decades.

Sacramento is the oldest incorporated city in California. It has had some form of city council since 1849, but prior to 1971, only four women had served on the council: Luella Johnston, elected the first year women could vote in California elections (not national ones) to a two-year term in 1912; Mary B. Lindley, who served a two-year term starting in 1922; Elizabeth Welch, who served out her husband's term when he joined the military during World War II; and Sacramento City College president Belle Cooledge, elected to the city council in 1947 and chosen by her colleagues to serve as mayor in 1948–49.

In contrast, since 1971 Sacramento has elected ten councilwomen, including two female mayors who were each re-elected to a second term, and six women to the county board of supervisors. In addition, women applied in record numbers to fill positions on appointive city and county planning commissions, parks and recreation boards, historic preservation boards, economic development committees, and arts organizations; and ran for elected positions on school boards and various service districts.

What caused these women to choose this place and time to move into leadership roles? What gave them the courage and strength to do it? And a bigger question—how did they they succeed? Because succeed they did! What do their experiences tell us that can offer guidance to women running for important posts today?

Societal Straitjacket

The first of the Sacramento female candidates in the 1970s and early 1980s were in their forties or fifties by the time they ran. That means that between the 1930s and 1960s, they learned how the world worked and what their designated place in it should be. In those decades, as community activist Kay Knepprath recalled, "It was just assumed that men would be in the important positions."

The particulars of "just assumed" can be seen in standard procedures used at the time. For example, the official population record, the U.S. Census, recorded the names of "head of household and wife of head." In case that didn't make clear where the power lay, a later question on the form asked: "What is the relationship of each person to the head of this household? (For example, wife, son, daughter, grandson, mother-in-law, lodger, lodger's wife.)"

The name of this household head was official. Married women took their husbands' surnames. In some cases, their own names did not even appear on documents; a woman was not Mrs. Jane Ellen Smith, but was instead Mrs. William D. Smith.

Language of the time coded the importance of males by using the word "man" as a generic word for humans. Thus, writing proclaimed that "all men are created equal;" books were titled *Man's Search for Meaning* or *The Rights of Man*; job labels were police*man*, mail*man*, fire*man*, chair*man*, and even council*man*; and street signs warned "*men* working" and "*man*hole cover." Our nation had "founding fathers," as though males ventured to the new world alone.

While the masculine was used for the generic, violations to that procedure occurred when descriptions obviously applied to the roles where females were herded. Thus, the boss was a "he" but the secretary a "she"; the doctor was a "he," the nurse, a "she"; the professor was a "he," the kindergarten teacher a "she." That the rules changed in such cases implied that the male version of words in all cases really meant a male. (Note: That "men" had a generic meaning was the basis of

Susan B. Anthony's attempt to vote in 1872. She argued that in the Constitution, the word "man" was used in the generic and thus included females. She was arrested.)

If women were not admitted to the circles of power such as the Sutter Club or the Rotary Club, where were they? At home. Susan Hauser reported in a Workforce.com review of women's roles, "Like it or not, girls growing up in the '50s would have been exposed to role models such as the housewives in *Leave It to Beaver, The Donna Reed Show,* and *Father Knows Best,* women whose career goals were getting the kids off to school and serving dinner on time." TV commercials portrayed women who were overjoyed by the whiteness of their laundry and encouraged them to make coffee like "good little Maxwell housewives." In their pretty dresses and white pearls, the TV moms cooked, cleaned, did laundry, and smilingly supported their husbands. So did women in textbooks. Teachers taught the girls to read, and Dick and Jane and baby Sally's mother showed them what a good woman does.

This homemaker role was appropriate for girls whose aspirations were inspired by Disney via *Snow White,*1937; *Cinderella,*1950; and *Sleeping Beauty,*1957. Each future princess was taught, "Someday my prince will come and I will be whatever he wants." When the prince finally did arrive, he took them to his home to support his life. Snow White did not rise up from her drugged sleep to advocate for safer additives to apples. Cinderella did not start a nonprofit to aid scullery maids. Sleeping Beauty did not file a #MeToo lawsuit. They lived whatever life Prince Charming required.

Toys trained girls to accept their position. When boys received gifts of trucks, bikes, and catcher's mitts, girls got Easy-bake Ovens, Suzy Homemaker appliances, baby dolls like Betsy Wetsy (whose greatest appeal was that she could wet her diapers), and, after 1959, Barbie, whose primary message was not about careers for women but about how a well-developed woman should look and what she should wear. And if girls failed to follow the rules? Old Maid cards threatened the answer.

Schools, as well, told girls how to be girls: wear dresses and take classes in home economics. Females were not allowed to wear pants to school, not even kindergarten girls dressing for snow. Home economics classes were regularly required for high school girls; there, young women learned to cook and sew rather than how to, say, run a city. Gwen Ihnat, in her series, *The Takeout*, described one typical 1950s assignment: "Adolescent girls would learn how to prepare eggs in a multiple of ways, because they didn't know how their future husbands would like them." Unless girls were in unusual school systems, they did not play sports. Federal funding for sports was used for male activities. Girls could lead cheers for the boys.

College-bound young women were teased that they were going for an "M-R-S" degree, and any woman supporting her husband through college might be awarded a jesting "Ph.T." for "Putting Hubby Through."

All young women did not instantly marry after school, of course. They might work for a few years. They could choose one of three careers: nurse, teacher, or secretary. Those three professions hired women. One example shared in this research revealed how quickly the lesson sank in. An elementary class had a guest speaker, an archeologist who regaled the class with fascinating stories of his time on a dig and the history his work uncovered. His talk enthralled the class, especially two young girls who listened with rapt attention. Later, when the guest had departed and the class turned to discussion, the teacher asked what careers students might choose for their own future. The girls' hands rose instantly. Called upon, they had the same response. Each breathed out with tremulous hope and excitement, "I want to be an archeologist's secretary."

Women were not just discouraged from entering other professions. They were essentially brainwashed to believe they lacked the ability.

Journalist Ann Curry recalls her entry into journalism in the 1970s. "I was told I couldn't be a reporter because women had no news judgment and couldn't carry the camera" (Pajer, 11).

Things did not improve for girls when they reached adulthood. Justin Beach wrote in *Women's Rights in the 1950s:* "In addition to facing family and social pressures to stay home, cook, and raise children, women's rights in the home were severely limited. In many states, women's property rights were still restricted. In other areas of the country, women could not make contracts, including wills. They also could not sell property, and in many cases, they could not control their own earnings. All of these were the legal right of the woman's husband or father."

Katie McLaughlin, writing for CNN, provided a list of limitations on women in these decades, commenting, "Can you imagine pregnancy being a fireable offense? How about job security hinging on your weight or the softness of your hands?" She listed these rather shocking limitations:

- **Women could not get a credit card.** McLaughlin notes: "In the 1960s, a bank could refuse to issue a credit card to an unmarried woman; even if she was married, her husband was required to cosign. As recently as the 1970s, credit cards in many cases were issued with only a husband's signature. It was not until the Equal Credit Opportunity Act of 1974 that it became illegal to refuse a credit card to a woman based on her gender."

- **In some states, women still could not serve on juries.** "It wasn't until 1973 that women could serve on juries in all fifty states" (McLaughlin).

- **Many university campuses did not accept women.** Yale and Princeton did not accept female students until 1969. Harvard didn't admit women until 1977. Texas A&M was all male until

1965. Columbia did not become coed until 1983. In California, at least, colleges were more open. California State Normal School, a precursor to the State College system, accepted women in 1862. The California State University system began accepting women in 1863. Stanford admitted women from the start in 1891. Moreover, all courses and majors, including the sciences, were open to women.

- **Women did not have equal opportunities at work.** Workplace equity is a battle women still face, especially in salary. Prior to the 1964 Civil Rights Act, women legally faced different requirements from males. McLaughlin provides the classic example faced by women working for airlines: "Stewardesses had to meet a certain height requirement, maintain a set weight, resign if they got married, maintain soft hands, and face mandatory retirement at age 32." One of this book's contributors could not be hired at a high school in Austin, Texas, because she had a child under one year of age, although male teachers could have children of any age.

Lest this depiction of female restrictions sound too grim, let's hear a round of applause for Nancy Drew, Jo March, and Diana Prince (a.k.a. Wonder Woman), fictional role models who lived lives of a more spirited sort. However unlikely her adventures, whatever challenges she faced, we can be sure Nancy Drew had no intention of being anyone's secretary. And give a nod to Alice, who fell into Wonderland, and Dorothy, whirled into Oz; they did not seek their unexpected adventures, but they coped and finally triumphed. The few role models that depicted girls doing more than keeping house or helping men planted their "girls can do it" seeds into fertile, ready hearts.

On a more mature level, and a more realistic one, a few actual women leaders also existed. Chief among them was former first lady Eleanor Roosevelt. At the 2019 White House Correspondents'

Dinner, historian Ron Chernow reminded the group, "Eleanor Roosevelt held her own press conferences, where she invited only female reporters. This proved a tremendous boon to women journalists across the country because even the most hidebound publishers realized they were now forced to hire women journalists." Always a strong leader, she continued to inspire community service long after her president-husband's death. Her influence was felt among Sacramento's trailblazing political women. For example, when Kay Knepprath moved out of her large family home to a smaller senior apartment, one of the items she took with her was a framed portrait of Eleanor Roosevelt, which she hung above her desk.

Of course, an outsider does not always see where inspiration enters the life of another person. When asked about her role models, in addition to Eleanor Roosevelt, Kay Knepprath listed Esther Williams, the swimming movie star. "She was an athlete," Kay explained. "She made it all look easy, but it wasn't easy. She was really an athlete." Today's girls have role models in tennis stars, victorious women's soccer teams, and incredible award-winning gymnasts, options females previously lacked in the sports world. Kay identified with the athletic skill when she saw it in movies.

As important as public role models can be, the influence of real people in our lives is generally the most powerful. In the backgrounds of many of Sacramento's women leaders dwelled powerful mothers or grandmothers, teachers, or mentors.

Glimmers of Hope

Though conditions were far from equal for women when Anne Rudin ran for city council in 1971, change was on the horizon. The historic battle for women's suffrage had demonstrated the power of women working together toward a goal. In 1966, the National Organization for Women was formed, primarily focused on achieving equal pay for women.

When women chose to take stances on specific issues, unifying a group was the standard technique. For example, the fight for clean air was initially led by women living in the smog of the Los Angeles basin in the mid-1950s. Cars had produced such high levels of air pollution that lung disease was becoming common and asthma rates for children soared. Margaret Levee, the mother of one asthmatic child, gathered eight friends in her living room to consider what could be done. They came up with the name Stamp Out Smog (SOS). Soon they had set off a movement. At a 1954 protest meeting in Pasadena, 4,500 citizens demanded a county grand jury investigation into why nothing was being done to curtail smog. Outside on the street women and children, some wearing gas masks, marched to call attention to the problem. They provided a glimpse into a world where women were influential (Steve Swatt, Susie Swatt, Rebecca LaVally, and Jeff Raimundo, *Paving the Way—Women's Struggle for Political Equality in California*, 2019).

In the late Sixties, the Equal Rights Amendment (ERA) was introduced in Congress. It read: "Equality of rights under the law shall not be denied or abridged by the United States or by any state on account of sex." It had been introduced before (the first time by Alice Paul in 1923), but this time the Amendment had traction. The House approved the measure in 1971, and the Senate in 1972. California was an immediate endorser in 1972. Although 35 states endorsed the Amendment, ratification required 38 states, and it ultimately failed. The fight for it, however, brought attention to the disparity between male and female conditions. (The 15 states that did not ratify the Equal Rights Amendment were Alabama, Arizona, Arkansas, Florida, Georgia, Illinois, Louisiana, Mississippi, Missouri, Nevada, North Carolina, Oklahoma, South Carolina, Utah, and Virginia.) Finally, in 2019, the state of Virginia approved the ERA, while urging extension of the ratification deadline.

In 1972, the Education Amendments Act passed. Title IX of that Act provides: "No person in the United States shall, on the basis of sex, be excluded from participation in, be denied the benefits of, or be subjected to discrimination under any education program or activity receiving Federal financial assistance." That is legal language for requiring schools to offer girls' programs equivalent to those offered to boys. Its principal impact was on sports programs.

Then in 1974 Congress passed the Equal Credit Opportunity Act, ending much of the discrimination against women in obtaining credit. The statute "makes it unlawful for any creditor to discriminate against any applicant, with respect to any aspect of a credit transaction, on the basis of race, color, religion, national origin, sex, marital status, or age," and "applies to any person who, in the ordinary course of business, regularly participates in a credit decision, including banks, retailers, bankcard companies, finance companies, and credit unions." This was an enormous step in eliminating the anonymity and dependence of women in a male-dominated society.

Entertainment media reflected these changes, very mildly at first. Susan Hauser noted that on TV, "A working woman as role model didn't come along until the late 1960s and early 1970s with shows such as *Julia*—where Diahann Carroll starred in the first non-stereotypical network TV role for an African American woman as Julia Baker, a single mom who worked full time as a nurse—and *The Mary Tyler Moore Show*—in which Moore portrayed Mary Richards, a career-oriented single woman who is a news producer for a TV station in Minneapolis" (basically, a nurse and a secretary, but still…). January of 1972 saw the first issue of Gloria Steinem's *Ms. Magazine*, a publication dedicated to discussions of equal rights for women. Perhaps the most obvious media symbol of the changing era was Helen Reddy's song, "I Am Woman," which touted the emerging power of women and won a Grammy Award in 1973.

I Am Woman, Watch Me Vote

The stage was set. Girls raised in the '40s, '50s, and '60s, who had been taught to keep house, cook well, be good mothers, and who were mostly confined to nursing, teaching, and secretarial jobs, were poised to assert their womanly wisdom in the '70s by leading grass roots organizations and running for local elective office.

In 1970 Sacramento was a mid-sized city. It had a population of 254,413, encircled by sprawling Sacramento County with 650,000 people (including the city). Nestled between the snowy beauty of the Sierras and the splashing seacoast of the Pacific, it was the heart of the rich agricultural valley that runs down the center of the state. The city is the capital of California and the county seat for Sacramento County.

From its earliest days, the city grew by welcoming diverse citizens. It has its roots in the gold rush, followed by the powerful influence of being the western hub of the transcontinental railroad. Both of these brought an influx of newcomers into the area who became residents. The area has long ties to descendants of hopeful dreamers mining for gold; merchants and farmers eager to settle down here; White, Black, and Brown migrants coming to escape the Depression and make a new start; Chinese immigrants who originally came to build the railroads and stayed to reclaim wetlands and build our extensive levee system; Japanese who came to farm and suffered the tragedy of internment in World War II; Hindu, Filipino, and Mexican farmworkers; and countless other visionaries from around the world.

In modern years Sacramento was labeled "the most diverse city in the United States" (Stodghill and Bower). In 1970, the county was home to State of California government offices, the Sacramento Army Depot, Aerojet Corporation, McClellan Air Force Base, and Mather Air Force Base, all of which drew new residents seeking work. The varied population called for insightful leaders with a strong vision of what the city could become, and the female activists who competed to lead Sacramento offered such a vision.

Many of the women mentioned in this book were not native-born Californians; like so many others, they came to the state as children, young wives, or students, yet their devotion to their adopted home was unstinting. And their love of Sacramento continued long after they left the spotlight of appointive and elective office.

Why Local Government Matters

Most people don't think about "local government" until their garbage isn't picked up; or they find they need a permit to make a minor improvement to their home; or police officers and sheriff's deputies begin to look more dangerous than helpful. The way citizens are treated at the local level leaves a lasting impression about all government. As the late Speaker of the House of Representatives Thomas "Tip" O'Neill said, "All politics are local."

The term local government refers to the first tier of governance and includes school districts, special districts, towns, and cities, as well as counties. The purpose of these entities is to deliver services to the public in an even-handed way. The underlying assumption is that it is more efficient for people to band together to get things done than to do everything individually. For example, rather than every household making a weekly trek to the garbage dump, they agree to pay a small fee to have the garbage picked up by the city or county where they reside. Among the services provided communally, local government deals with roads, traffic and transit planning, housing, economic and community development, job training, social services, environmental protection, recycling and solid waste, sewer service, delivery of safe and dependable water, parks and recreational amenities, youth services, libraries, fire protection and emergency medical help, municipally supplied energy, airport planning and administration, law enforcement, flood control, and maintenance of accurate voter rolls and administration of fair elections. Generally, there is little dispute about the wisdom of people taxing themselves to provide such community services.

Planning for how city and county land is to be used is a little trickier. While most people want to live in a safe and attractive community, opinions may differ as to what land uses should be allowed and in which locations. Notions of property rights and freedom from government intrusion are often in conflict with notions of the general public's good.

Professionally trained planning staff advise city and county officials about the overall vision (or general plan) for the community's growth, as well as specific plans for land use in each community planning area, often including several distinct neighborhoods. Planning concepts or blueprints are usually arrived at through consultation with the public, including "stake holders" such as neighborhood associations, advocates for environmental and historical preservation, social services groups, property owners, and business and professional groups. In an advise and consent process, formally appointed advisory committees and planning commissions consider the ideas of professional staff, developers, and citizens before they forward their recommendations to the city council or board of supervisors. Plans are codified through the zoning ordinance, which specifies allowable uses for each property, including where residential, commercial, industrial, and agricultural uses may occur, as well as the placement of parks, schools, libraries, and community centers. The zoning ordinance may also specify lot size, building placement, density, and height restrictions; the zoning ordinance also sets up a process for considering exemptions.

Advisory committee and planning commission meetings are often the first place where citizens encounter their government in action. Local officials are often seated in a judicial manner at a dais elevated above the audience. Citizens wishing to address their representatives may have to overcome shyness or even fear to trudge up to a podium, speak into a microphone, and make their case. If the public is not treated with courtesy, including the full attention of the officials, and if their points of view do not appear to be considered fairly, the stage is set for citizen contempt for all levels of government.

The City of Sacramento, founded in 1849, is the oldest incorporated city in California. In 1920 voters adopted a municipal constitution, or City Charter, which sets policies and procedures for how the city governs. Although amended periodically, the City Charter is surprisingly short, clearly worded, and relevant to issues affecting citizens one hundred years later.

Both the city and county have professional management staff that serve and advise the elected officials on matters of public interest, including an annual budget. The top appointed city officials are the city manager, city attorney, city treasurer, and city clerk. The mayor is elected by all city voters, while the eight members of the City Council are elected by district in staggered elections. Members of the non-partisan City Council and the mayor serve four-year terms, and currently represent about a half million city residents. Three women have served as mayor in the city's 170-year history: Belle Cooledge, who was named by her City Council colleagues to a two-year term, and Anne Rudin and Heather Fargo, elected by voters, each serving two consecutive four-year terms. In addition to electing the mayor and city councilmembers, city voters elect board members to the Sacramento Municipal Utility District, where women's influence has also been notable.

In a structure similar to the City of Sacramento, the County has a charter that empowers the Board of Supervisors to adopt ordinances, zone properties outside incorporated areas (outside the cities of Citrus Heights, Elk Grove, Folsom, Galt, Isleton, Rancho Cordova, and Sacramento), establish programs, levy taxes, and appropriate funds. However, counties do not have the broad powers of self-government to generate revenue granted to cities. Another major distinction between the cities and counties is that county voters elect a sheriff, district attorney, superior court judges, an assessor, and members of the county board of education. For the most part, the Board of Supervisors does not have direct control over the sheriff, district attorney, or superior court judges. However, some oversight is granted through the watchdog role of the civil grand jury system to investigate allegations of misconduct, conduct audits, and investigate detention facilities. The County Board approves a county executive responsible to the Board of Supervisors, who plans, organizes, directs, and coordinates county activities. The five members of the non-partisan Board of Supervisors are elected to four-year terms in staggered elections. The Board of Supervisors elects its own chair and vice-chair annually.

Laws, procedures, and protocols are in place to insure the efficient operation of local government. But appointed and elected representatives are the living face of government. If those faces do not reflect the citizenry itself, local government—and all government—will founder. With the entry of women into public positions in growing numbers, local government began to mirror society as a whole.

FEMALE MEMBERS OF THE SACRAMENTO CITY COUNCIL

(Thirteen Elected, Three Appointed)

The Pioneers: 1912-1950

Luella Johnston 1912-13

Mary B. Lindley 1921-23

Elizabeth "Buffy" Welch 1940s (Appointed)

Belle Cooledge 1947-51; Mayor 1948-50

The First Wave: 1971-2008

Anne Rudin 1971-83; Mayor 1983-92*

Callie Carney 1976-77 (Appointed)

Lynn Robie 1979-92

Eva Garcia 1982-83 (Appointed)

The Hon. Kimberly J. Mueller 1987-92

Lyla Ferris 1987-92

Heather Fargo 1989-2000; Mayor 2001–08

The Second Wave: 1993-2019

Deborah Ortiz 1993–96

Lauren Hammond 1997–2010

Bonnie Pannell 1998–2014

Sandy Sheedy 2001–12

Angelique Ashby 2011–

* Because Sacramento changed from odd-year elections to even-year elections in 1992, eliminating the 1991 election, Anne Rudin was mayor for nine years.

FEMALE MEMBERS OF
SACRAMENTO COUNTY BOARD OF SUPERVISORS

Sandra Smoley 1973–1992

Illa Collin 1979–2006

Muriel Johnson 1993–2004

Roberta MacGlashan 2005—2016

Susan Peters 2005–2020

Sue Frost 2017–

ALSO IN THIS BOOK

Christy Anderson

Sarah Aquino

Paula Boghosian

Jeanie Bruins

Linda Budge

Pamela Bulahan

Susan Carlsen

Christina De La Cruz

Michele Gish

Frances Gracechild

Jane Hagedorn

Keri Howell

Collette Johnson-Schulke

Pam Johnson

Kay Knepprath

Ann Kohl

Paige Lampson

Marion O. Lawrence

Carolyn Martin

Congresswoman Doris Matsui

Eleanor McClatchy

Diana Madoshi

Porsche Middleton

Joyce Mihanovich

Virginia Moose

Stephanie Nguyen

Dr. Barbara O'Connor

Barbara Payne

Speaker of the
House of Representatives,
Nancy Pelosi

Suzanne Phinney

Marylou Powers

Suri Pulipati

Ruth Rippon

Jean Runyon

Estelle Saltzman

Jeanie Shaw

Tracy Martin Shearer

Sophia Scherman

Karolyn Simon

Bobbi Singh-Allen

Jo Smith

Marge Tomczak

Kathryn Uhl

Iva Walton

Jaci White

Susan Willoughby

Effie Yeaw

CHAPTER TWO

Role Models, Aspirations and Life Changing Events

We must respect each other and be kind to each other.
—Sacramento Congresswoman Doris Matsui,
World War II Japanese-American internment camp survivor

The ways girls are raised, societal norms and the events of the times certainly have a bearing on the adults they later become. But sometimes girls and women look around and say to themselves, no, that is not who I will be. Sometimes they even vow to change the world if they ever have the chance.

Mayor Anne Rudin, Councilmembers Lynn Robie and Lyla Ferris, County Supervisors Sandra Smoley and Illa Collin, as well as Kay Knepprath were all born during the Great Depression and suffered deprivations like millions of others. But the economic struggles of their parents and grandparents did not lead them to self-pity. It taught them to persevere against all odds.

Reflecting on their childhood role models, both Illa Collin and Kay Knepprath mentioned their grandmothers, who had very strong and generous personalities. Kay's maternal grandmother lived with Kay's immediate family, as well as with her aunts and uncles, during the Depression years. As an only child of two working parents, Kay confessed that she needed supervision. Also as an only child, Kay relished the company of her cousins when she accompanied her grandmother to their rural homes. Describing herself as a tomboy, Kay quipped that since she lived in Kansas City, she "climbed billboards instead of trees."

Kay Knepprath explained that she has always been drawn to issues of social justice. Recalling that she volunteered in a Kansas City soup kitchen once a week after high school during the Depression, she said such volunteer work wasn't required by anyone, "It was just something I felt compelled to do." When Kay was an adolescent, she realized the shocking truth of how mean spirited racial prejudice was in segregated Kansas City, Missouri, where a neighborhood restaurant posted a sign in the window refusing to seat and serve Blacks. Admitting that both sexism and racism were a given during the late 1940s and 50s, that particular sign sickened her. It led to a heated argument with her racist uncle, and a life working to advance social justice, especially the right to decent housing in her adopted home of Sacramento beginning in 1961.

Lynn Robie might as well have been an only child, born 10 years after her nearest sister and 4 years after her brother, Roy De Forest. Lynn was born during an arduous Depression era road trip to flee poverty, drought, and a grasshopper plague in Nebraska. In the early 1930s, Lynn's father, a tenant farmer, and her mother, a fearless and domineering woman, loaded their three children with only the most necessary belongings into a Model T Ford pickup and headed west, sleeping on mattresses thrown over boxes in the back of the truck and earning their way, like so many other migrant families, by harvesting crops. Lynn was born midway through this journey in Grand Junction, Colorado. Also midway through the journey, as Lynn's mother looked on in horror, the truck, with her husband and children in it, began rolling backward toward the edge of a 1,000 foot cliff. She single-handedly moved a huge rock to a rear tire to prevent certain doom.

Once settled in the small town of Selah in Yakima Valley, Washington, Lynn grew up as somewhat the forgotten child, tagging after her older brother, Roy, who was remarkably tolerant of his sniffling little sister as they explored their new rural home. Lynn adored her father and was heartbroken at age thirteen when he died. Following her father's death, Lynn's mother did what all single mothers do: everything, including managing three care facilities. Lynn credited her brother for helping to instill in her a joyful, independent, and caring view of the world. Both were true originals. Roy would later be nationally recognized as one of Northern California's most innovative artists, known for his quirky autobiographical paintings and assemblages created during the Pop and Funk art eras.

Illa Collin greatly admired the independence and strength of her mother and grandmother. She spent her early years in poverty, living in a spartan house without indoor plumbing in the arid coal mining town of Rock Springs, Wyoming. Illa's alcoholic father died in a mining accident when Illa was 10 years old. After her husband's death, Illa's mother, Vivian, had to leave her two daughters in the care of a family friend while she served in the Cadet Nursing Corps during World War II, sending money home to support her two daughters. Deprivation and loss left deep emotional scars, but also gave Illa a profound empathy for victims of poverty, addiction, and abuse. Later, when Illa became a member of the Sacramento County Board of Supervisors (Second District), she was a vocal and effective advocate for social services for those in need of a helping hand.

Sandra Smoley was born near the end of the Great Depression and raised in an idyllic small town in Iowa, where her father was a doctor and owned a 24-bed hospital. Sandy began working as a nurse's aide at age 14 and earned her nursing degree in 1959. Recalling that her father ruled with an iron fist, Sandy credited both of her parents with instilling in her the importance of giving back to her community by volunteering. That became a life-long ruling principle in her life, especially after she came to Sacramento in 1961 at age 24, the wife of a young doctor and mother of two children. Smoley struck up a friendship with (future Supervisor) Muriel Johnson in Iowa City in 1959, a friendship that has lasted six decades.

Barbara O'Connor never ran for elective office, but her influence as a teacher, mentor, public policy expert, technology leader, and behind-the-scenes playmaker was formidable. She was born in Midland, Texas, and after her parents' divorce, Barbara moved with her mother and sister to Los Angeles to live with her paternal grandmother, whom she counts as the most influential person in her life. Remembered as one of the smartest and most curious people O'Connor has ever known, her grandmother was loving, "kind and non-judgmental until you crossed her or lied to her. And then she was your worst nightmare...My grandmother believed I could do anything I wanted to." (Jo Chandler, *Sacramento Magazine*, 11/2/06). O'Connor became a high achiever in school and in her professional life. She attended the University of California at Los Angeles (UCLA), majoring in music, the first in her family to graduate from college. She was planning to attend law school when she discovered debate at California State University at Northridge. She loved it, joined the Northridge debate team in 1969, and became one of the few women debating on the national stage. Her analytical and persuasive skills soared.

Teaching was one of the few professions society found acceptable for girls in mid-twentieth century America, in part because it is a nurturing, caring profession. As a young girl, Lyla Ferris's dream was to be a teacher, but she was also inspired by the indomitable spirit of Nancy Drew, fictional girl detective. Advised by many that she was "too nice to be in politics," she nevertheless followed her convictions, finding strength to run for office from the love of family, friends, and her church. As the oldest of seven children, Ferris had a deep and personal empathy for the poor, having been raised on welfare by her twice-divorced mother.

Motivated by the same social conscience that inspired other female community leaders, Lyla quietly and doggedly worked as a community organizer in the Del Paso-Robla neighborhood, where she raised five children. Recognizing early on that the needs of her community were being ignored by city government, she served on the Del Paso-Robla Neighborhood Council, Youth Development and Delinquency

Prevention Project, Sacramento Economic Community Council, and Sacramento City Planning Commission. This experience prepared Ferris to run for the school board in her community and, later, the city council.

Sacramento City Councilwoman Kim Mueller, who at age 31 was elected to represent District 6 in 1987, was born in Newton, Kansas, and raised in Grinnell, Iowa, where her father taught high school and her mother held an administrative job at the university. The oldest of three girls, she excelled academically and loved being a Bluebird and Campfire Girl, never feeling homesick while at summer camp. Her parents gave her ample freedom to question and explore. In her senior year of high school, she received a scholarship from the Rotary Club that enabled her to be an exchange student in South Africa. At age 17, Kim flew to South Africa unaccompanied, excited to see a whole new world. The experience profoundly altered her world view.

Raised by parents who were civic minded pacifists, Kim was deeply influenced in her views about public service by the teachings of the Mennonite and Congregational Church. While serving on the City Council, Kim emphasized constituent services, responding quickly and thoroughly to issues brought to her by the voters. Among her top policy initiatives were protection of the environment, addressing HIV-AIDS in a tolerant and scientific manner, historic preservation, campaign finance reform, and advancement of the arts.

Life Changing Events

As a twelve-year-old girl riding bareback across the dry, treeless plains near her home in southwest Wyoming, Illa Collin knew little about the war raging halfway across the world and even less about the Heart Mountain Relocation Camp in northern Wyoming where Americans of Japanese descent were imprisoned. She was stunned when a college friend told her about the camp. She explained, "I couldn't believe what I was hearing. I said, 'You mean U.S. citizens were locked up without due process of law?' I asked my history teacher about it and he said, 'We don't teach about that. You'll have to go to the library and look in the archives to see what the president required.'" After that research, she wrote her U.S. senator and received a letter back encouraging her studies. She made a vow to herself: "I told myself if I'm ever in a position to do something about that, I will."

Motivations spring from many sources. Almost forty years later, in 1983, Illa was at the forefront of the push for letters of apology and reparations for Sacramento County employees of Japanese descent who had been sent to one of the camps. She was also a leader in the formation of the Sacramento Tree Foundation, a direct result of growing up in a town nearly devoid of trees.

Councilmember Lauren Hammond recalled that, "We all have defining moments in life that help shape who we are, what we believe, and what path we choose to travel. When the Watts riots exploded (1965), I was 9 years old and living in Los Angeles. My dad could not cross the line of tanks on Crenshaw Blvd. to make his way home. That night, I vowed to do all I could to make a difference in people's lives."

Not all adult actions trace back so directly to a person's childhood, yet signs of a social conscience appear frequently in the lives of Sacramento's female leaders.

Mayor Heather Fargo was raised in a traditional middle-class family and was expected be a good student and excel at college. Her role models were her mom, a mother of three who made sure her three children did their homework and had a supportive home and school life; her father, an administrator for three California cities; and her teachers. She loved reading biographies and was particularly impressed with the life of Clara Barton. In 1971, Heather was on track to attend college at the University of California at Santa Barbara when the debilitating effects of scoliosis, first diagnosed when she was twelve years old, became severe enough to require surgery to correct the painful curvature of her spine. This required her to drop out of college after just two semesters. She endured surgery and was immobilized in four separate body casts, spending nearly eight months mostly alone. One particularly Medieval contraption that Heather described as "the Rack," stretched her from her hips to her chin "until my eyes almost bugged out." To achieve the limited mobility of turning over, her body cast was fitted with spokes attached to two wheels that allowed her to turn over. In 1972 she transferred to the University of California at Davis and graduated in 1975 with a degree in Environmental Management and Planning, which she said, "combined my love of nature and people." Heather said that she "never regretted" the decision to undergo surgery (followed by walking casts), pointing out that, "It gave me the chance to do everything that followed."

The patience, endurance, and determination that Heather developed at age eighteen would serve her well when she later ran for elective office in Sacramento and faced an even more debilitating medical challenge while she was mayor: multiple sclerosis.

Compassionate Regard

Four of the women described in this book were trained as nurses, a profession that is still widely viewed with admiration and trust by the American public. They are Anne Rudin, Sandra Smoley, Lynn Robie, and Karolyn Simon. Their natural compassion, capacity for listening, and ability to make fact-based decisions made them effective representatives and leaders of local charities, appointive boards, and elective bodies.

Anne Rudin received her nurses' training in Pennsylvania and taught nursing for several years. After moving to California with her husband in 1948, Rudin became active in the League of Women Voters, employing her talent for attentive listening while she gained leadership skills, eventually rising to the position of President of the California League.

Former City Councilmember Lynn Robie (age 80) at 2015 Kaiser Nursing School reunion of 1957 graduating class, wearing original cap and cape

Lynn Robie earned her nursing degree in Oakland, California, in 1957 and was assistant instructor of nursing there from 1957–60. After Robie moved to Sacramento, she served as Nursing Director for the groundbreaking federal program, Head Start, from 1965 to 1967, housed at the Women's Civic Improvement Club in Oak Park. The need for quality childcare was a personal challenge for Lynn as well, so she brought her young son with her to attend pre-school at Head Start's Play Space. Her son was the only White boy at the school, which helped him reject racial stereotypes as he grew up. Later, Lynn's nursing and communications skills would be put to work at the American Lung Association of Sacramento-Emigrant Trails, where, as Smoking Cessation Director, she wrote the nation's first smoking cessation curriculum for young people, published in 1987.

Karolyn Simon earned her nursing license in New York in 1963, followed by a master's degree in Biology in Connecticut in 1967. Her knowledge and love of the natural world and people guided her in her work in Sacramento, where she advocated for protection of the environment and the people who live in it.

Sandra Smoley brought her compassion as a nurse and her personal health struggle to her role as the first woman to be elected to the Board of Supervisors in 1972. In 1985, Smoley publicly announced her battle with breast cancer, thereby helping to overcome the stigma that had kept breast cancer and the search for a cure in the shadows. Recalling the attention given to her decision to have a double mastectomy, she commented, "I had my breasts on the front page of *The Bee* day after day. I'm just glad I didn't have cervical cancer!" She was also a vocal and visible supporter of the Susan G. Komen Breast Cancer Foundation and its drive to raise awareness, promote mammograms, and find a cure.

CHAPTER THREE

Training for Leadership

I don't think we recognized the power of what we were doing at the time.
—Jane Hagedorn

Women Organize

Long before there was social media, crowd funding, the Internet, or even telephone answering machines, women found ways to get together and get things done. In the 1960s and 1970s, women got together to address the social, educational, environmental, economic, racial, political, and cultural issues of the time by meeting in the living rooms of the hostesses. Using a "telephone tree," mimeograph machines, and the U.S. Postal Service, they got the word out and, working as volunteers, achieved amazing results for the betterment of society.

In Sacramento, women formed and joined women's groups such as the Tuesday Club, the Junior League, the Women's Civic Improvement Club, the League of Women Voters, the American Association of University Women, the Creative Arts League, Soroptimist International of Sacramento, the National Council of Jewish Women, the Medical Auxiliary, and other women's groups, sometimes organized in support of male-run organizations.

Of course, women also formed committees as co-equal partners with men to affect the course of local history in such civic-minded groups as the Urban League, National Association for the Advancement of Colored People, Sacramento Concilio, the Japanese American Citizens League, the Parent Teachers Association, the Red Cross, United Cerebral Palsy, the Sacramento Children's Home, the Sacramento Alliance for the Mentally Ill, the Sacramento Symphony

League, the Save the American River Association, the Sacramento Tree Foundation, the Sacramento Audubon Society, the Environmental Council of Sacramento, the Sierra Club, United Way, Republican and Democratic clubs, as well as countless other committees formed under the umbrella of organized religion.

Female community activists wrote books, published pamphlets, organized cultural programs, made speeches, created documentary films, and appeared before male-controlled city councils, boards of supervisors, school boards, arts organizations, and advisory groups to advocate for change throughout the '60s and '70s.

Two examples of how women's committees were used to tackle major issues are provided by the leadership of Jane Hagedorn, Carolyn Martin, and others in saving Sacramento's vanishing Victorian homes, as well as advocating for the preservation of native oak trees in the Sacramento Valley and California as a whole.

When her attention was drawn to the alarming rate of demolition of Sacramento's irreplaceable Victorian buildings, Jane Hagedorn invited a group of women, including AAUW leader Carolyn Martin and historic preservation advocate Paula Boghosian, into her living room to analyze the problem and come up with a plan to save them. The result? In 1973, after doing extensive research and documentation, the Sacramento Branch of American Association of University Women published a book titled, *Vanishing Victorians—A Guide to Historic Homes of Sacramento,* that raised public awareness and paved the way for new laws to save historic structures.

Jane also recognized the value of native oaks in our region, not just for their beauty, but also for their natural ability to cool in hot Sacramento summers, improve air quality, reduce energy consumption, absorb noise, increase privacy, and provide food and habitat for wildlife. Native oak woodlands once graced much of California, but vast groves of valley oak, blue oak, black oak, interior live oak, coastal oak, and the rare oracle oak were being lost at a rapid rate, cut down to make room for new subdivisions or to clear land for agriculture.

Jane recalled, "One of the things we did, again in my living room, was write a book on native oaks." The book, *Native Oaks—Our Valley Heritage*, published in 1976 by the Heritage Oaks Committee, was a guide to the botany, planting, and care of native oaks in the Sacramento Valley. Created by volunteers skilled in writing, editing, photography, and teaching, the book raised public awareness of these living monuments, many that predated the arrival of settlers during the Gold Rush. The community-based campaign led to adoption of local ordinances to protect Sacramento Valley native oaks. Later, in the mid-80s, Hagedorn and fellow volunteers took their native oak education campaign statewide in an attempt to convince other California cities and counties to adopt heritage oak ordinances. In 1988 a statewide private non-profit group, the California Oak Foundation, was formed to conserve and preserve our oak tree heritage.

Hagedorn, Martin, and Ann Kohl were also instrumental in forming the Environmental Council of Sacramento (ECOS) in 1971. ECOS is an umbrella organization that initially comprised representatives of the American Lung Association of Sacramento-Emigrant Trails (ALASET), the American Association of University Women (AAUW), the League of Women Voters (LWV), the Sierra Club, the Audubon Society, the Ecology Information Center, and the Medical Society. The combined membership of these organizations was a powerful tool of persuasion when appointed and elected officials debated how to address issues of suburban sprawl, loss of agricultural land, and degradation of the region's air and water.

The successful use of committees to agitate for change was a recurring theme in the '70s and '80s. A poignant example of one individual who overcame enormous odds to become one of the most well-loved and effective advocates for persons with disabilities was Frances Gracechild. As a survivor of polio when she was a child,

Gracechild became a fierce advocate for the rights of the disabled and seniors. With passage of the Rehabilitation Act of 1973, California established 29 Independent Living Centers throughout California. Sacramento's Resources for Independent Living, established in 1976, was led by Gracechild from 1984 to 2017. Her advocacy for the disabled before local boards, commissions, and elected bodies was distinguished by her dignity, warmth, and flawless preparation.

The League

Conversation among Sacramento's female leaders often started with a question: "How long have you two known each other?" As such queries are wont to do, this brought up recollections.

"I was the president of the League the year that Kay joined, so—"

"So, when did you join the League, what year? When were you president?"

"I was president . . . what year were you president?"

"We had two-year terms—"

"I think it was '61, '63."

"My mother was president of the local League in 1959-60. Anne Rudin attended her first Sacramento League meeting at our house in Hollywood Park. I was just 13 years old!"

"I joined the League when Anne was president."

"The League" in this discussion is the formidable League of Women Voters (LWV). Founded by suffrage leader Carrie Chapman Catt when women were on the verge of winning the right to vote back in 1920, the League was established because, as the League's official website states, "a nonpartisan civic organization could provide the education and experience the public needed to assure the success of democracy." The League of Women Voters was a place where women were welcome at a time when other options were limited. Information-focused and nonpartisan, it became a training ground on public policy issues for Sacramento's future female leaders.

The Sacramento County LWV describes its task as "educating voters and empowering citizens to have an active voice in government." Given how many of Sacramento's female political leaders emerged from League membership, the local chapter can consider itself highly successful at that task. Anne Rudin, Lynn Robie, Illa Collin, Kay Knepprath, Joyce Mihanovich, and Virginia Moose were members. They learned to analyze and dig deep into the reasons for, and possible effects of, proposed laws and ordinances at the federal, state, and local level. The League's public policy position states directly that "LWV does not support or oppose candidates or political parties." It may, however, support, oppose, or remain neutral (take no position) on measures.

Kay Knepprath provides an example of how the League operated to expand knowledge. "The League was studying any number of issues, including the environment, and that got us involved with other organizations that were environmental organizations, and with other leaders of those organizations. My first League study was poverty, co-chaired with the woman whose husband was a pastor in Oak Park. My experience with the League of Women Voters whetted my appetite for working for change." Because League positions are arrived at after extensive study and are written with great care by committees, their formal positions continue to be seen as strongly credible.

Anne Rudin's story of joining the League reflected the position of many young mothers after World War II:

I got married in Philadelphia. My husband was a medical student there. He had already been accepted in a hospital in L.A. for an internship. So we moved there. And then he was called into the service. He had to pay back an Army Specialized Training Program; he went to school on that. He got a three-year residency in Palo Alto. We lived in a Quonset hut; I loved it. We couldn't get a car. You couldn't get a car then. I had three kids at home and was so bored with no one to talk to.

I had to do something. And to do something of value. I wanted something that had to do with issues. Women couldn't join partisan groups if their husbands were working for the government. I saw these women coming from something at the next Quonset hut to ours. They said they had been to a tea at the League of Women Voters. I said, 'Is that Democrat or Republican?' They said it was non-partisan.

And that's when she joined. She added, "I had no babysitter. We used to just help each other."

The plight of educated competent women finding themselves bored and isolated with young children at home was also recounted by Christy Anderson, Susan Carlsen, and Karolyn Simon. Anderson, who began working as an attorney in the Sacramento City Attorney's office in the early '80s, had "two under two" when she first learned that League meetings were being held in her south Sacramento neighborhood. When she realized that she could bring her babies to the meetings of the Southgate Unit, where childcare was provided, she was ecstatic. This might cure her of what she later learned was postpartum depression. It was at the Southgate Unit meetings that Anderson first met Councilwomen Anne Rudin and Lynn Robie, Supervisor Illa Collin, and activist Virginia Moose. The elected women continued to attend local LWV meetings as their schedules permitted, encouraging and helping younger women. It was Collin who first encouraged Anderson to apply for a job with the City Attorney's office.

Likewise, Susan Carlsen joined the Southgate Unit soon after she moved to Sacramento from North Carolina in 1976. Eager to study public policy issues in depth, Carlsen dove into the League's study of "solid waste management," an alternative approach to trucking endless mountains of garbage to local landfills. Carlsen was profoundly impressed by the public policy knowledge of Collin, Rudin, Robie, and Moose, who encouraged her to go to law school. When she agreed to take a chance and apply, Councilmember Anne Rudin wrote a glowing letter of recommendation for her. With a little help from her friends in the League, Carlsen changed her life course, practicing law in Sacramento from 1985 to 2012.

Simon had three young boys, including twins, when she first moved to Sacramento from New York in 1973. Starved for intellectual stimulation and adult conversation, Simon was drawn to the fledgling environmental movement and played a leadership role in the Environmental Council of Sacramento (ECOS). Though she wasn't a member of the League, Simon became lifelong friends with the League members who began running for local office in the '70s.

Retired Supervisor Illa Collin's compassion for the plight of young mothers grappling with loneliness and diminished self-esteem after having children was deeply personal. Collin suffered postpartum psychosis after the birth of her third child and considered killing herself and her children before successfully getting mental health treatment. As Supervisor, Illa was a stalwart supporter of County funding for mental health services and was opposed to cutting funding during the budget crisis of the early 2000s. "'If you've ever been poor ... or really needed mental health services, then you know that cutting these programs has a real impact on people's lives," Collin said. "These are usually the kinds of budget decisions where I go home at night and cry.'"(Robert D. Dávila, *The Sacramento Bee*, 12/29/2002)

Photo courtesy of Sacramento League of Women Voters

Illa Collin, Sacramento LWV president, 1973-1975 and member of the Sacramento County Board of Supervisors, 1979 -2007

Gaining Experience

Being active in the League of Women Voters was but one of the many ways the candidates and those supporting them had prepared themselves for government service through the years. Each of them

HAVING IT ALL

The challenge of "having it all"–building a career while also bearing most of the burden for childcare and domestic chores–has proved to be grueling for many women. Before licensed childcare became more widely available, women in groups such as the League of Women Voters helped each other with childcare. They also formed childcare co-ops and those that could afford to do so hired babysitters or found childcare in private homes, often unlicensed. A 1977 study of San Francisco day care providers found that just 40 percent were licensed and proposed that California counties be tasked with setting up licensing procedures. In Sacramento, the Childcare Coalition, a local committee of childcare advocates, found a sympathetic ear in Supervisor Illa Collin, who took the lead on the Board in support of strengthening the County Children's Commission and Childcare Coordinator position in the early '80s. Key leaders who advocated for more accessible childcare included Jaci White and Marge Tomczak.

Finding affordable, accessible, quality childcare and early learning opportunities continues to be a huge issue for women. In 2019, under the guidance of Sacramento's vice mayor, a working group composed of six organizations presented the City with recommendations to increase access to and address the lack of affordable childcare. The problem of affordability was especially acute in Sacramento in 2019, where the average annual cost of full-time care for an infant was $14,200. A single mother earning the median income of $60,000 could expect to pay 23% of every dollar earned on care for each child (*The Sacramento Bee*, 8/22/19).

Securing paid family leave for a period following the birth of a child was also a stubbornly elusive goal, when in late 2019, the federal government finally approved 12 weeks of parental leave for the country's 2.1 million government employees. Approximately 80% of workers in the private sector still have no access to paid family leave. According to an Associated Press article, "Just 9% of wage earners in the bottom 25% have access to paid family leave, according to the U.S. Bureau of Labor Statistics. That compares to 30% of wage earners in the top 25%. Meanwhile, millions of construction workers, retail workers, public school teachers, warehouse and transportation workers, and restaurant employees have to forego paychecks to take time to care for a new child" (Alexandra Olson, Associated Press, *The Sacramento Bee,* 12/23/19).

had already, long before running, developed a personal commitment to serving the community.

For most of the women, the process started early. Illa Collin recalls collecting cans and bottles during World War II when she was a girl. Decades later, Kim Mueller began the same way: "I was picking up litter when I was at junior high. I was part of the recycling club in high school. Every Friday afternoon, we'd gather boxes all over the high school and we'd get together and we would sort it." She began walking the precincts in Des Moines in 1972 for George McGovern's presidential campaign before she was old enough to vote. Kay Knepprath volunteered in a Kansas City, Missouri, soup kitchen during the Depression. Many of Sacramento's trailblazing political women chose the helping professions of nursing and teaching.

Although Sandra Smoley did not use her nursing degree professionally after she came to Sacramento in 1961, she became a tireless volunteer for the Junior League, the Symphony, Red Cross, United Cerebral Palsy, the Children's Home, and United Way, ultimately rising to the position of president of each organization. Long before she decided to run for the Board of Supervisors at age 34, she had observed the path aspiring men took in gaining prominence and recognition. Male business leaders, newly arrived in Sacramento, invariably joined the boards for the Symphony, United Way, and Boy Scouts. As a volunteer, Smoley had built a network of contacts, male and female, who respected her intellect, her organizational skills, and her commitment to the community. She recognized that her experience as a volunteer prepared her well to run for local office.

Many elected women built their resumes by forming committees and serving on the boards of local community organizations and government appointed commissions. Anne Rudin, for example, was the League's representative on the City Charter Revision Commission, the group that recommended changing the city council election process to electing by districts. Lyla Ferris was elected to the Robla

School Board. She notes, "School boards—that's where most women start, even today." Illa Collin was appointed by Governor Jerry Brown to the state Reclamation Board. Kay Knepprath became involved with historic preservation, was president of the Sacramento Old City Association, and advocated for decent and fair housing for all.

Lynn Robie's understanding of government processes grew out of her community work. "My son was in an Oak Park preschool, the Playmate Preschool; I became their nurse." By the time she ran, "I'd been helping with public health in Oak Park for years." Back then, Oak Park had a less than stellar reputation. "People asked my husband, 'Why do you let her do that?' Ron said, 'We don't 'let' her do anything. She does whatever she wants.'"

By the time Robie ran for City Council, she was able to post a list of "20 years of community service." Her list of accomplishments included the traditional (and usually male at that time) committee roles such as chairperson of the Sacramento County Parks and Recreation Commission, a member of the Sacramento Regional Area Planning Commission, and a board member of the Sacramento Science Center and Junior Museum. She also noted being a member of the P.T.A., a qualification that reached out to an audience of mothers, suggesting her experiences were in line with theirs.

Like Robie, Bonnie Pannell was also deeply involved in her community and understood its issues. She became acquainted with city government as the wife of a politician; her husband Sam Pannell, was the City Councilmember for District 8 from 1993–98. Mastering the issues that came before him, she was readily elected to replace him at his untimely passing after five years on the council. She wrote, "I have lived in District 8 for 38 years and worked hard over the past thirteen years fighting to bring new developments, jobs, and growth to our community." She subsequently served for sixteen years.

Lyla Ferris's activism began after her 30-year marriage ended in divorce. Her five children were older and "I was by myself," she explained. "My first political experience was campaigning against Prop 13. We had to make cuts—school nurses, library services; it was pathetic. It's never been really fixed."

Lynn Robie laughed as she added, "You'd be surprised how many cupcakes you have to sell to fill that gap."

Ferris was a community organizer for a pilot program, Youth Development and Delinquency Prevention Project. "That was a time I was really involved in the community. I went door to door in Del Paso Heights. I was out there, that was my job. People knew me. I was a church member in North Sacramento." She lost the first time she ran for school board, but the next time she ran, "I got elected. And they sent me to a school board convention in Miami. They had 'wives' programs' while all the business was conducted. I was one of a few women delegates." Asked if she was assumed to be someone's spouse, rather than a delegate, she replied with great emphasis. "Oh, yes!" She added, "Once I was elected to the School Board, I joined the California Elected Women's Association for Education and Research (CEWAER). It was a relatively new statewide group for all elected women. Anne Rudin was a founding member, and it was there I met her. She became a supporter and a role model for me."

Heather Fargo learned about government service by a very different path. Her father had been city manager for Davis, Santa Maria, and Stockton, California. She had watched the process of managing cities from the perspective of a child. While in junior high school, Fargo ran for class treasurer and edited the school newspaper, and in high school joined the debate club. "I loved it and was good at it (and it was a good thing to have taken, it turned out). We debated other schools, and it required a lot of research and strategizing."

After she moved to South Natomas, Fargo encountered the reality of debate gone awry in the passage of California's Proposition 13 in 1978, which curtailed property taxes for vital local services. "I had expectations. I had read the plan. But we were one of the first post-

Prop. 13 communities and the city had no money. We didn't get traffic lights or stop signs, didn't get libraries; parks weren't being developed. Our little community association we thought would just be for social activities turned into an advocacy group. We ended up speaking in front of the City Council a lot. I once spoke at 35 public hearings in one year."

Was she ready for this? She recalls, "Unlike many women who went into politics, I did not serve on a PTA, and was not a member of the LWV or the AAUW or any other women's organization." But her experiences growing up had prepared her well. Fargo was instrumental in the formation of the South Natomas Community Association in 1980, and in 1981 she served on the County Tree Task Force, which put her in a space to expand her commitment to environmental issues. She sat on the board of the Environment Council and, with Karolyn Simon, served on a city board to update the city's Master Plan for Parks and Recreation. She added that her professional training and experience in environmental planning and management led to practical strategies for managing the fallout from Prop. 13. "I also helped form the Revenue Sources Management School based at UC San Diego to help train park and recreation staff in raising revenue and doing the marketing necessary to keep the doors open and services provided despite major budget cuts due to Prop 13. I learned so much about cities, counties, and parks during that time that became so useful once I was elected."

Photo by Larry Dalton

Councilmember Deborah Ortiz and Mayor Heather Fargo, 2004

Deborah Ortiz, a Sacramento native, described her deep connections to her Oak Park community, including a wide network of friends from elementary school, high school, college, and law school. Her subsequent work for the non-partisan State Legislative

Counsel's office honed her analytical skills and her later work for Assemblyman Richard Polanco gave Ortiz valuable experience in Democratic politics, including campaigning. Explaining that legislative staffers often spend their vacation time working on campaigns, Ortiz related how she was thoroughly schooled in the importance of well-staffed phone banks and ground games. When she decided to run for City Council, she had the skills and local support necessary to run a competitive grass roots campaign. In the five person race for Council in March 1993 she was the top vote getter in a winner-take-all special election (held to fill the remainder of Joe Serna's term after he was elected mayor).

Mentors & Supporters

The value of an experienced and trusted adviser is hard to overstate. In many ways, Sacramento's trailblazing political women mentored one another. Trusted advisors also functioned in the background, including Jean Runyon and Barbara O'Connor. When asked for her advice to future politically-active women, Dr. O'Connor's first recommendation was "Get a mentor," describing her own growth through her relationships with Jean Runyon and others. Her second admonishment was, "Men are allies." It's a position the women interviewed for this book often acknowledged, citing particularly the valuable advice they received from former City Councilmember Lloyd Connelly and past Mayor Phil Isenberg.

In 1981, as women began to develop political influence in the city, a group including Runyon, O'Connor, Knepprath, Ray Butler, and McGeorge School of Law Dean Gordon Schaber, founded The Harry S Truman Club, organized in support of local Democratic candidates, both female and male. Regular luncheons and discussions provided mentoring in the form of practical advice and information sharing, as well as discussions of new ideas and promising trends in business and government.

Movers, Shakers and Witches

Whoever sets the agenda usually gets what she wants accomplished in the meeting.
–Gloria Feldt, *From Oppression to Leadership; Women Redefine Power*

"I have someone I want you to meet!" she said with her beguiling smile and a twinkle in her eye. For over 50 years, **Jean Runyon** was Sacramento's most powerful and effective liaison for business interests, arts organizations, charities, local politicians, and aspiring young people. If there was somebody she wanted you to meet, you didn't pass up the chance.

Born in Concordia, Kansas in 1927, Jean Hamilton was the only child of track and field coach Brutus Hamilton and Rowena Thornburg Hamilton, an actress in the Chautauqua Theater circuit. Jean adored her father and was deeply influenced by his work ethic, as well as his brilliant writing and storytelling. When Jean was five years old, the family moved to Berkeley, California, where Brutus coached the University of California (Cal) track and field team. Blessed with a great deal of freedom to explore during her childhood, Jean loved sports, excelled at music, was an avid reader, and became more and more drawn to the theater. A romantic from the get-go, Jean fell in love with fellow Cal student, Mercer Runyon, and at age 21, married him and moved from the Bay Area to his Courtland ranch in the Sacramento River delta. But the monotony of farm life, cooking, cleaning, and raising her son and daughter 22 miles south of Sacramento were not enough for ebullient Jean.

In the late 1950s Jean took the first step in building what would later become a public relations powerhouse in Sacramento. A chance encounter with Eleanor McClatchy, president of McClatchy newspapers from 1936 to 1978, led to a job planning theater parties for the summer Music Circus in Sacramento. The theater!

Often compared to theater legend Carol Channing, whose high breathy voice charmed millions, Jean Runyon harnessed her empathy for people, her creativity, her fine intellect, and sometimes zany sense of humor in order to put people together and accomplish one goal after another.

In 1976 she teamed up with young journalist Estelle Saltzman to form the Runyon Agency, Inc., a public relations firm of 15 women. It took four more years for the agency to hire a man. Jean explained that, "It was only women for a while because our receptionists were frequently promoted and men never applied for that job in those days."

Estelle agreed to manage the finances of the firm, which were subject to Jean's unbridled altruism. Estelle learned that when a good cause captured Jean's heart, "She would give away her money, your money, anybody's money." At one point Estelle quipped, "We should rename the firm: Runyon Saltzman, a not-for-profit corporation."

These are the words that came to mind when Estelle remembered Jean, who passed away at age 82 in 2009: generous, intelligent, magnetic, caring, dynamic, natural, a phenomenon, and a mentor. The recollections of friends, family, and colleagues compiled in an *In Memory of Jean Runyon* book, paint a picture of a woman who was not only bigger than life, but who also made virtually every person she met feel that they were the most important person in the world. It was never about her ego. She always had time to listen and help.

Helping in one case meant buying just the right outfit for a young woman who was running for the elective board of the Sacramento Municipal Utility District. As the only woman in a field of black-suited male candidates, her "powerful red" suit boosted her confidence and helped her come within 100 votes of being elected.

Another example of Jean's unfiltered compassion is described by her stepdaughter, who accompanied Jean (then in her seventies) to a meeting that didn't adjourn until 10:00 p.m. Driving through a rough part of town, Jean noticed a middle-aged man walking down the street, falling down drunk, accompanied by an adolescent girl. Worried for their safety, Jean pulled over and offered them a ride. Jean was unfazed that the man was bleeding all over her white leather back seat. She gently asked the man's daughter for directions to their house and delivered them safely home.

But there was nothing prissy or sanctimonious about Jean Runyon. She laughed at racy jokes and pulled off some outrageous pranks, especially on April Fool's Day. One such prank targeted an important east coast client, the president of Best Products. The company had a store on Arden Way with the novel distinction of having a large section of the building motorized and on tracks, dubbed The Notch. On April 1, Jean called the company president and solemnly informed him that after it had been turned on that day, The Notch had picked up tremendous speed, careened off its tracks, and barreled into three cars on Arden Way. Expletives from the east coast ensued until Jean announced, "April Fool's!"

Dr. Barbara O'Connor, CSUS communications professor and telecommunications policy expert, marveled at Jean's encyclopedic knowledge of a vast array of subjects. "Jean had a mind like a steel trap. She was an early version of Wikipedia." Runyon and O'Connor became great friends and advocates for women in business, the arts, education, and government.

In a world replete with insensitive male chauvinist gaffes, in 1962 Jean Runyon graciously accepted an award for Public Relations "Man of the Year," and in 1987 welcomed the chance to be the first woman accepted as a member of The Rotary Club of Sacramento. Rather than fret over their non-acceptance in the all-male Sutter Club, Jean Runyon, Anne Rudin, and Carolyn Reid co-founded the Sacramento Women's Club, which later evolved into the Sacramento Women's Network. They knew that the co-operative spirit of women making connections would advance society in general.

Jean Runyon getting ready to ascend to her rooftop for Halloween, 2005

Jean Runyon's professional and volunteer schedule didn't allow much time for domestic chores and she admitted that she was no Julia Child. But she had good intentions. The one time she was inspired to cook a nice roast beef dinner for the family, she set the kitchen on fire. But if Jean didn't soar at cooking, she soared as a witch every Halloween for over 30 years, climbing onto the roof of her home decked out as a wicked witch, cackling with glee as she threw candy down to wide-eyed children trick-or-treating below. Her love of Sacramento was symbolized by such moments of unrestrained glee.

Inspired by Jean's Halloween antics, her friend and the first woman to be elected to the Board of Supervisors in 1972, Sandra Smoley, brought the wicked witch to her own rooftop, where she dazzled neighborhood trick-or-treaters for 27 years. The Halloween witch was reincarnated in Supervisor Muriel Johnson's neighborhood after she was elected to the Board in 1992. In addition to their creative delight in Halloween, Runyon, Smoley, and Johnson were also ardent supporters of the arts, including the Sacramento Symphony, the Crocker Art Museum, and the Sacramento Theater Company.

Two politically savvy "go to" women who worked for decades behind the scenes were Virginia Moose and Karolyn Simon. Virginia Grether Moose, born in Berkeley in 1926, graduated from U.C. Berkeley with a degree in economics in 1947. She moved to Sacramento in 1957, where she promptly joined the League of Women Voters, eventually becoming close friends with Anne Rudin, Lynn Robie, and Joyce Mihanovich. Virginia put her degree in economics to work as treasurer for Rudin's and Robie's campaigns, as well as for the Sacramento County Democratic Central Committee for over 20 years. Virginia was elected as trustee of the American River Flood Control District in 1996 and served four terms. She was a board member of the Sacramento Area Flood Control Authority (SAFCA), served as an appointed member of the Sacramento Housing and Redevelopment Commission, and was a member of the Sacramento Compensation Commission. A strong advocate for environmental protection, Virginia also offered her wisdom and expertise to the Environmental Council of Sacramento (ECOS).

Karolyn Simon was the very definition of "play-maker." Born in 1941 and raised in Olean, New York, Karolyn Webster Simon moved to Sacramento in 1973, where she quickly became a leader in ECOS, using her organizational skills and persuasive powers to give voice to local non-profit groups and individuals who normally didn't stand a chance against powerful special interests. So savvy were her political skills that *The Sacramento Bee* named Karolyn Simon as the third most influential local government lobbyist in 1980, a spectacular achievement for an unpaid community activist up against lavishly paid lawyers and lobbyists.

Like Virginia Moose, Karolyn served on the Housing and Redevelopment Commission and the American River Flood Control District, where she was elected chair for 21 years in a row. Her community service also included the Sacramento Employment and Training Agency, the City Parks Commission, and Private Industry Council.

Another behind-the-scenes woman of influence is Collette Johnson-Schulke. While not directly involved in the local election campaigns of Sacramento's trailblazing women, she was, like Jane Hagedorn and Jean Runyon, a mover and shaker, skilled at bringing people together to advance new ideas and solve problems. Collette's professional trajectory was as a government relations liaison for local, statewide, and national associations of realtors; then District Director for Congressman Bob Matsui for eight years. More recently, she worked for over 13 years as legislative liaison for Sutter Health, working with the City and a myriad of interested parties to get the new Sutter Hospital built downtown. By actual count, Collette attended 52 meetings with stakeholders before plans for the hospital were finalized and accepted by the City.

Born in 1943 in Aurora, Illinois, to Irish-immigrant parents, Collette admitted to pushing the limits while in high school. After attending Marquette University, she married and was later divorced in 1975. Facing the daunting task of supporting herself and her two children, Collette began selling real estate in Pacific Palisades in Southern California. After remarrying and living in several other communities, Collette found her true home in Sacramento as a liaison working to get things done.

Recollecting her first meeting at City Hall in the '80s representing the Board of Realtors, Collette didn't quite know what to expect and was taken aback when she realized that she was the only woman seated at a conference table dominated by men. It was a welcome relief to discover the support and networking opportunities provided by Soroptimist of Sacramento and the rapidly expanding Sacramento Women's Network.

Whether working behind the scenes or in formal electoral settings, all of the women covered in this book worked together to promote good government and their vision of a community that works for everyone.

Tipping the Scales

Running for an elected office does not automatically follow from earlier community activism. What tipped the scales toward running? Illa Collin's answer was one of timing. "I'd already been involved in a lot of decision-making. I decided if I'm going to make a difference,

I had better run now because the seat was opening up. I'll do it now, I thought, and I could make a difference in the decisions the Board would make next term."

Heather Fargo also ran for election to make a difference. She wrote, "I held no offices in school or college. I never took a class in political science. I never planned to run for public office—until I got mad. In 1988, just ten years after moving to Sacramento, I decided to run for City Council and was elected in 1989." What led to that decision? As her advocacy on behalf of good planning and adequate services for South Natomas began to take more and more of her time, she began to realize, "If I was sitting up there [on the Council dais], I could do more."

Many of Sacramento's influential women preferred to work behind the scenes and could be described as playmakers, plotters, and schemers who preferred to stay out of the limelight; encouraging and helping the women running for office, while advocating for causes important to them. Kay Knepprath observed that women often seek the advice of others, form committees, and strive to reach consensus before putting their ideas into action. Asked why she never ran for elective office, Kay Knepprath quipped, "I couldn't picture myself sitting at a dais." She made a valid point. At City Hall, members of the City Council sit above the assembled public at an elevated, highly formal dais. This physical arrangement separates and intimidates, not everyone's preferred way to relate to her fellow citizens.

Having no incumbent to oppose is a good time to run. Joyce Mihanovich had to remind Lynn Robie of what initially caused her to run. "You said you wouldn't run, and then Bob Matsui was elected to Congress," leaving a vacancy on the Council. (Congressman Robert Matsui was elected to Congress in 1978 and re-elected for thirteen terms, serving until his death in 2005. Born in Sacramento, he was six-months old when his family was sent to a Japanese American internment camp in 1942.) Robie's candidacy was not entirely incumbent-free. The man who was appointed to fill the remainder of Matsui's City Council term, based on the promise that he would not run for election, reneged on his promise and ran anyway. He came to regret that decision.

Kim Mueller had walked precincts for Lloyd Connelly and other candidates. One of them, Ed Smeloff, told her, "You like to walk precincts, you should run for office." She acknowledged, "It had never occurred to me. It really had not. I think by that point I had taken the LSAT, because all I could think of for further education was a law degree. But I didn't really know that I was learning by doing."

Sandy Sheedy's path to elective office was unusual. After her husband, County Supervisor Ted Sheedy, retired, following 16 years of service on the Board, she was looking forward to spending more time with him. But one evening in 2000, Mayor Joe Serna called her: "I want you to run for City Council." Surprised by the summons, Sandy said she'd think about it. "Fine. I'll call you back in an hour." Ted had been alerted prior to Joe's call and told Sandy, "I don't think you have a choice."

Although Sandy Sheedy had served two years on the City Planning Commission, she felt no desire to run for local office. However, she seized the moment and, assisted by a professional campaign consultant, waged a grass-roots campaign, walking the precincts of District 2 three times. This was the same district Lyla Ferris had represented from 1988 to 1992. Despite Ferris's victories for her district, it again suffered from official neglect of basic public services, such as streetlights, code enforcement, maintenance of bridges and parks, and city efforts to revitalize business districts. Sheedy set out to fix the neglected infrastructure and rebuild relationships with her fellow citizens.

It was while Sandy was campaigning that she first witnessed the dire results of poverty and landlord indifference. Knocking on the door of a rundown house, she was told that there was mold everywhere, including a room where a young child slept. When she saw firsthand the magnitude of the problem, she immediately called City Code Enforcement and started the process that required the landlord to make needed repairs. During her twelve years as a City Councilmember, Sandy never lost sight of her role as a woman and an elected official. "Kindness, listening, assistance, and help. That's what we're there for."

Sandy Smoley saw a run for political office as a reasonable next step after serving on the boards of directors of eight prominent community organizations, including as president of United Way of Greater Sacramento and chairwoman of the Sacramento Metropolitan Chamber of Commerce Health Committee. Smoley's first campaign for Board of Supervisors (Third District, 1972) took an unusual turn when the powerful men of her party (Republican) wrote her off as a viable candidate. Supervisor Patrick Melarkey, a Democrat, had suggested she run for Supervisor since her a strong interest in health and welfare issues—the purvue of the County—would serve the board well. During the primary she faced seven male rivals, including six Democrats, none of whom made it to the runoff. Left with two Republican candidates, the political insiders of her party had already begun celebrating the expected victory of her male rival, when Smoley was approached by the local Democratic organization, who suggested they help manage her campaign. The previous support for her six Democratic rivals was shifted to Smoley (who was viewed as the lesser of two evils) and she won handily, serving on the Board for the next 20 years.

While Sacramento's influential women did not necessarily share the same views on issues, they had the same views on responsible government, on how people should be treated, and they shared a desire to make things better. Commenting on the women she worked with, Councilmember Sheedy noted that women "stick to the basics." Like Sheedy, Supervisor Smoley stuck to the basics by regularly meeting with her constituents in the diverse neighborhoods of her far-flung district. Noting that the folks in Rio Linda, Elverta, and North Highlands were just like the people she grew up with in Iowa, she understood that "All they want is for their electeds to be among them and one of them."

CHAPTER FOUR

Campaign Strategies

Working together we can prove that grassroots campaigning is still effective in the city of Sacramento.

—Lynn Robie, May 1979

Sitting in her office high up in the Robert T. Matsui U.S. Courthouse, District Judge Kim Mueller recalled her entry into the Sacramento political world. It was 1981. She had a brand new B.A. from Cal Poly Pomona and was completing a summer internship with the California Agrarian Action Project in Davis. "I just showed up at [Councilmember] Lloyd Connelly's office, and I said, 'I'm volunteering.' And they said, 'What are you willing to do?' and I told them, 'I'm willing to do anything.' They said, 'Are you willing to walk precincts?' and I said, 'Yes.' Not everyone's willing to walk precincts, you probably know that, but that's how you get to voters' issues—and those could be stop signs, speed bumps, landscaping—neighborhood issues. It's taking care of the local, local things."

Walking the Precincts

Walking the precincts. It was the mantra of Sacramento's successful women candidates. Meeting the voters face to face. Speaking to them directly. Listening to what they had to say. Joyce Mihanovich recalled, "I used to take a day off work every week and walk the precincts." Lynn Robie nodded vigorously. "Me too. When I ran each time [she was elected to three terms on the city council], no person opposing me did that. I walked every single precinct there was. District 8 was huge. I walked and my supporters walked. I didn't know about Meadowview and I walked it. I sure did."

Clearly, when the process of electing city council members changed to the new eight-district system, campaign strategies for winning a seat on the council had to adjust, too. For the voters, choosing their City Council representative was no longer a matter of selecting their favorite from a citywide slate. And for the candidates, raising funds from the well-heeled to advertise their names, faces, and positions on city-wide issues was no longer the key to victory. Instead, candidates needed to reach diverse voters in distinct neighborhoods of the city.

Although districts are adjusted after the U.S. Census count every ten years to make them equal in population size, that does not make them equal in issues; and to be successful, candidates had to identify and address concerns in their own district. For example, what the post-Proposition 13 South Natomas suburb demanded was not necessarily required for the classic, stately Land Park; and certainly, the less-wealthy Oak Park and Meadowview areas had different needs than East Sacramento, with its older homes and "Fabulous Forties" mansions. Smart campaigners went directly to the voters they hoped to represent in order to identify and discuss the issues that mattered to those voters.

Door-to-door campaigning is not everyone's cup of tea. Consider the options: trudging through Sacramento's notorious "dry heat" or through the occasional rain and mud, legs aching, heels blistered, stomach growling, knocking on strangers' doors (behind which might lurk a belligerent citizen with a growling Rottweiler), explaining a candidate's position over and over and over—versus, say, spending a few quiet, air-conditioned hours at the latest movie—which would you choose?

The women candidates and their teams chose to walk the precincts. One clear message offered by the women candidates to voters over and over, and *delivered personally,* was that these candidates would be in touch with their constituents and wanted to hear about their needs.

The primary advice Lyla Ferris gives to anyone wanting to serve is, "Do the groundwork. Know the community and its people." Lynn Robie gave an example, "We did a lot of stuff with schools in Meadowview. I made a point of meeting every one of the teachers."

Walking the precincts was not just about talking. It was listening. Mueller recalls: "I remember many times when I was walking in my district, I was young and there were a lot of people my age now [early sixties]. There were times when the woman in a couple would come to the door and she would say something like, 'Well I think it is time for a woman.' Then there were times when an older man would come to the door and he would say, 'You're too young to be running for City Council.' And I would say, 'Well, that's up to you to decide. But what issues do you care about?'"

A general dissatisfaction with the prior election system had motivated the change to city districts for council representation. The feeling was that at-large councilmen had not been attentive to their less wealthy constituents. Lynn Robie noted, "They lived in Land Park. Meadowview was in terrible shape. When we started, I don't think those men ever went and saw people."

The women candidates were changing that. So significant was responding to district issues that in one campaign flyer Robie wrote: "Dear Neighbor, I have walked the neighborhoods of District 8 for the past three months. I have listened to your views and I am determined to work for you to make your community a better place to live." She also pledged to "remain open-minded on issues and seek community advice." She then gave specifics of where she would put her efforts if elected, based on what she had learned from voters while walking the precincts. Her list included such mundane tasks as to "improve garbage and refuse pick-up," as well as the more optimistic challenge to "provide more parks and recreation programs" and "increase job opportunities." (When the Meadowview area finally got a dog park, by the way, they named it the Lynn Robie Off-Leash Dog Park.)

Photo by Ron Robie

Retired Councilmember Lynn Robie at 2014 ribbon cutting ceremony for the Lynn Robie Off-Leash Dog Park

The candidates and their supporters generally walked in teams, and these alliances helped build their lasting friendships. They walked the precincts *with* one another and *for* one another. Mueller initially walked with the candidate she supported, Councilmember Lloyd Connelly. "I was just a young volunteer, and they said, 'Okay, you're walking the precinct with the candidate.' He would walk one side of the street; I'd walk the other side. It was thorough, and it was exhaustive."

One of the favorite stories of the first wave of female candidates and their supporters was the time they were campaigning for Supervisor Illa Collin. At the end of a long hot day of walking the precincts, they met together to share experiences and exchange information, only to realize the candidate herself was missing. Concerned, a few of the group backtracked, looking for her. Kay Knepprath recalled, "Well, we found her. There was Illa sitting in a voter's house downing a beer." Even those who didn't experience that particular evening nodded. "Oh, yeah. That sounds like Illa."

An alternate version of walking the precincts was the coffee klatch, where voters would welcome a candidate and a small gathering of neighbors into their homes for conversation. Lyla Ferris remembered the skill with which Anne Rudin engaged people. "She'd come to your house for coffee klatches and was extremely effective. If only one or two people showed up, she was calm and greeted them and went on as if twenty were there. She was always so elegant." Again, the focus was on getting information as well as giving it.

A Little Help from My Friends

The campaigning women were each other's strongest supporters. Today, memories among the women are filled with the unifying term *we* and with references to one another's actions. They say: "We did Anne's election first, then Illa's," and, "Then you got elected and we helped Anne get elected mayor. Then we helped Lyla to City Council. We helped Karolyn."

People who support the same candidates generally have similar values and, working together, develop friendships. Reflecting back, Lynn Robie and Joyce Mihanovich recalled their early days. "We met at Illa's campaign," Lynn said. Joyce remembered, "We [she and her husband] had run Fred Wade's campaign, and my husband met Illa. He and Illa were both from Rock Springs, Wyoming, so that was instant connection."

Many candidates had a "kitchen cabinet" to advise and coordinate their campaigns. The shared joke was that they certainly were not in the kitchen. In the early days of campaigns for Anne, Lynn, and Illa, they met in the 926 J Building, a warren of small offices dubbed the "good government ghetto" because so many low budget nonprofit groups had offices there.

The women gave fundraising parties for each other. They lent their names and their popularity to other candidates. They relied on staff or volunteers from each other's campaigns. Virginia Moose, for instance, was treasurer for multiple city council candidates as well as for the Sacramento County Democratic Central Committee. A list of individuals working on a campaign for Illa Collin includes a pool of familiar names: campaign manager, Lynn Robie; office coordination, Joyce Mihanovich; communications, Kay Knepprath; fundraisers, Virginia Moose; finance, Jane Hagedorn; issues, Lloyd Connelly; analysis, Tony Mihanovich. Looking back on their time in office, more than one former City Councilwoman recalled the scrapbook compiled by Lynn Robie documenting her successful campaign. Kim Mueller still cherishes her own scrapbook.

When Lyla Ferris was defeated in her run for a second term on the City Council in 1993, she became Administrative Assistant (AA) to Illa Collin, replacing Joyce Mihanovich. Though the Supervisor and her AA worked quite happily together, the similarity of their names posed a recurring problem. "People would call up and ask to speak to Illa [pronounced Eye-la]," Ferris recalls, "and I would say, 'This is Lyla [pronounced Leye-la], and they would think they were talking to Illa." It didn't help for the women to use their middle names. "She was Illa Mae and I was Lyla Kay," she laughed.

Support from a women's group was a tried-and-true technique for Sacramento women, beginning with the first woman elected to the City Council, Luella Johnston. She ran and was elected in 1912, when California women could vote on city and state issues, even though nationwide suffrage for women was years away. Luella had been president of the Tuesday Club, initially a literary gathering that morphed into a political support group. Nicolas Heidorn detailed what happened next in his book, *Luella Johnston, California's First Councilwoman:* "In 1904, Luella organized a coalition of thirty women's clubs into the Women's Council." Heidorn noted that they did not organize to back a candidate, but to work for city improvements such as a new high school, street electrification, public drinking fountains, residential mailboxes, and building a public swimming pool. But when she ran for office, Luella had a ready group of supporters.

Dive into My Campaign

Swim, eat, chat with friends, and support your local candidate—what more could an afternoon offer? The "social media" of the 1970s and 1980s was an invitation to a gathering. Come meet the candidate. Share a burger and a handshake. The invitations, many designed by local graphic artist Jo Smith, were clever and drew supporters. One invitation for Virginia Moose for SMUD Board, for example, was for a "Formal Swimming Party" in which attendees were invited to "Wear your formal swim wear or your waterproof formal wear." Those invited were given choices for responding: "I'm diving in to support Virginia," or "My formal suit is at the cleaners, but I want to keep in the swim with a contribution."

One strong campaign strategy was to provide lists of those who supported the candidate. Given the smaller range of individuals in a district (rather than in the city as a whole) people named were likely to be known and, ideally, influential. One flyer mailed out in May 1982 from "Friends of Illa Committee" invited those who received it to a "Women for Illa Collin Luncheon." The flyer provided "a partial list" of female sponsors— four columns of names with 38 women in each column. It comes as no surprise to see among them Anne Rudin, Lynn Robie, Karolyn Simon, Jane Hagedorn, Kay Knepprath, Virginia Moose, and Joyce Mihanovich.

Advertising material of the time had an informal tone. Lynn Robie promised that she was "willing to research issues and return your phone calls." Lyla Ferris proclaimed, "I will return your phone calls!" One of Illa Collin's appeals said, "We need you!!!" and offered the respondent a checklist of options to return:

- Organize and/or hold neighborhood coffee hours
- Put up a lawn sign at my house
- Work on a lawn sign crew
- Be an office go-fer
- Work on mailings—the staplin', lickin' crew that works odd hours
- Make the supreme sacrifice and walk precincts and/or my neighborhood
- Help on special events
- $$$ always needed and appreciated

An even less formal appeal by Illa was headed, "It takes more than money," and gave respondents a checklist beginning, "I will help Illa by:"

+ Licking envelopes
+ Walking precincts
+ Putting up a lawn sign
+ Telephoning
+ Hosting a party or coffee
+ Any old thing that's needed

One helpful step was when candidates got endorsements from *The Sacramento Bee* or the *Sacramento Union*. For example, the *Union* wrote in 1979: "Lynn Robie, 43, is a registered nurse who has attracted broad support in the community as she waged an energetic grass-roots campaign for the 8th District seat that Robert Matsui relinquished last year in order to run successfully for Congress." The editorial then described Robie's service to the community, ending with a recommendation for her election to the City Council.

Public Appearances

Do clothes make the woman? It depends on your point of view. Constraints on women entering the all-male bastions of state and local government were almost Draconian in the late '60s and early '70s. After being appointed by Governor Jerry Brown to serve out the term of a former member of the State Reclamation Board, Illa Collin appeared at her first meeting wearing pants instead of the customary skirt or dress. There was a practical reason for this, besides simple comfort. Illa had begun bicycling extensively in Sacramento, delighted by the fresh air and gorgeous canopies of street trees. But the men on the board objected to her attire and admonished her not to show up at any future State Reclamation Board meetings wearing pants. Illa wore pants anyway.

Collin was always an independent spirit, eschewing make-up and declining to fuss too much over her hair. As Illa's first campaign heated up in 1978, her good friends and advisors began to worry about her electability and proposed a make-over. A new haircut and business appropriate clothing were tried, even though Illa resisted the change, insisting "I'm in. Take me or leave me." The make-over didn't stick and Illa stuck to her non-conformist ways. Illa was elected seven times, serving 28 years on the Board of Supervisors. The electorate didn't seem to think that "clothes make the woman."

Anne Rudin wore light make-up and displayed a conservative but feminine fashion sense, and—despite the demands of her position—sewed many of her own clothes. She drew the line when she was told that a make-up artist would apply heavy make-up prior to a scheduled TV appearance. "Absolutely not," she firmly but politely insisted.

Kim Mueller faced a different challenge: she looked too young, an unlikely candidate walking the precincts. "What I did was I went to J.C. Penney's, I got my 'City Council Candidate outfit.' The skirt and the blouse with the right scarf. I wore pumps because I was not going to look young. I did walk with Karolyn Simon, who wore tennis shoes. She was older and distinguished."

Credit: © Genaro Molina/Sacramento Bee/ ZUMA Press Wire

Kim Mueller holding campaign walking shoes following her election to Sacramento City Council in 1987

Expectations

Societal expectations and gender biases run deep. When Anne Rudin arrived at her first official meeting of the Sacramento City Council in 1971, it was assumed by her all male colleagues that she would make coffee. No, she didn't.

But, in truth, it was hard to let go of her nurturing nature. For years, Anne rushed home before her Tuesday evening Council meetings to make dinner for her husband, whose medical condition required three balanced meals each day.

Not so for Illa Collin, who was first elected to the Sacramento County Board of Supervisors in 1978. Illa didn't cook, but her husband Don was an excellent cook. "If the kids came home and heard popcorn popping, they knew that I was cooking dinner," laughed Illa. Her culinary repertoire reached its peak with chili and finished with coffee.

Expectations regarding food are complicated. Councilwoman Sandy Sheedy grew up in Colusa, a tiny agricultural town north of Sacramento, where her father was manager of a sportsman's club and her mother was a beautician. On the odd occasion at the end of the month when the family's budget was tight, her mother scrambled eggs, onions, and peas for dinner, a special treat for Sandy. Unaware of its tight budget origins, Sandy introduced the dish to her husband, Supervisor Ted Sheedy (1971-87), who still views the dish as delectable.

Male expectations can act like blinders. One of the duties of Mayor is to greet notable guests to the city. One such guest was the actor Donald O'Connor, invited to be guest of honor for a screening of *Singing in the Rain,* marking the November 1986 re-opening of the Crest theater as a revival movie house on K Street's new transit/pedestrian mall. Mayor Anne Rudin graciously appeared at Sacramento International Airport to welcome O'Connor, who brushed right past her as he searched the entourage for the expected male mayor.

Local press coverage also exhibited a subtle bias. Sandra Smoley recalled that, when reporting on the official acts of the Board of Supervisors, Sacramento newspapers usually featured the name of the male Supervisor who took the lead. If it was Smoley who led her male colleagues, invariably she was not mentioned; the official act or decision was attributed to the whole Board of Supervisors.

A prominent land use attorney ruefully admitted to misjudging Lynn Robie by violating a tradition and professional courtesy given to Councilmembers. Generally, there is some deference given to Councilmembers regarding proposed projects in their district. Shortly after she took office, Robie found herself on the losing end in an 8 to 1 vote approving a project she was against, a stinging act of collegial disrespect and an embarrassment. Following the Council meeting, Robie tapped the attorney on the shoulder, advising him that he would get to know her well and he would never make the same mistake again. The project was never built.

Heather Fargo recalled that after her first election as Mayor, the city manager had the annoying habit of walking into her office unannounced and without knocking. "He never would have done that to Joe Serna," her predecessor.

On the other hand, neither Deborah Ortiz nor Sandy Sheedy ever felt dismissed by their male City Council colleagues because of their gender and believed they were on an even footing, especially, Kim Mueller recalled, once a councilwoman had demonstrated her ability to count votes.

Re-elections

The strategy for re-election campaigns was easy. Do what you said you would do, then make sure the voters know about it.

"The one thing you can say about Lynn Robie, she was the Queen of Community Meetings," Robie recalled. "If there was a problem, we talked about it. I probably had a community meeting once a week." When Robie first won election, the citizens of District 8, which includes Meadowview, were angry after years of official neglect. She described sitting through meeting after meeting where people yelled at her. "I felt bruised," she says. But she kept coming, "Then pretty soon they stopped yelling at me, and we got some things done."

Meeting with constituents was a good strategy for solving problems. It also was a good strategy for informing constituents about the candidate's progress on their issues, progress that fueled reelection. Bonnie Pannell used her perseverance on reaching her goals as a reason for voters to re-elect her. She reminded voters:

I have been on the Sacramento City Council for thirteen years. Ten of those years, I've worked on South Line Light Rail Phase II (Blue Line to

> Cosumnes River College) and Delta Shores Development, a 600-acre
> project… Both of those projects will be completed in 2015. I want
> to complete what I started. I have three other major projects in the
> design phase on Bruceville Road: a water tower, a senior housing
> project, and a retail and housing project at Sheldon and Highway 99.

Illa Collin enjoyed lively public discussion at Board meetings. Reporter Bill Lindelof interviewed her for *The Sacramento Bee* as she neared retirement. "Collin said she has never been bored at a meeting because of the diversity of viewpoints shared by those who testified on so many matters. She said there have been some intense meetings, especially when the Board tackled the idea of building affordable housing throughout the county. The Board chambers were packed. 'There were hundreds of people all ready to lynch us,' Collin said. 'It could have been unruly, but each one of us on the Board in their own way told citizens that many people have died in wars to protect freedoms, including the freedom of speech. Freedom of speech means somebody listens and that you don't try to shout somebody down. You have discourse back and forth and then you come to a decision.'" Operating with such an attitude got Collin reelected to seven terms.

Kim Mueller practiced direct contact with voters. She related her system: "We adopted a process which is that you send a letter to the constituent, you send a memo to staff, and you dog it. And you don't let it go until the constituent gets some kind of answer, even if it's not what they want to hear. And that was the key to maintaining your seat. It's really what city councils are for."

Accomplishments are noted, contacts are made, meetings are held. But when the re-election campaign comes around and the incumbent once again faces opposition, the cycle returns, and it is back to walking the precincts.

CHAPTER FIVE

How They Led

Have Your Vision, Know Your Subject, Connect with People!
—Nancy Pelosi, Speaker of the House of Representatives,
Addressing women upon receipt of the LBJ Liberty and
Justice for All Award, 2019

Women have always found ways to obtain, exercise, and hold onto power. As Speaker of the House of Representatives Nancy Pelosi once counseled, "You go through the gate. If the gate's closed you go over the fence. If the fence is too high, we'll pole-vault. If that doesn't work, we'll parachute in." When asked how she obtained her power, Pelosi quipped that she didn't wait for it to be given to her, she seized it.

I Had an Awful Lot to Prove

Reflecting on her early days serving on the City Council, Anne Rudin said, "I had an awful lot to prove. I had to prove I wasn't militant," like Gloria Steinem. "When I first ran (1971), leadership was an issue particularly because I was a woman and there was a school of thought that there was just one model of leadership. She said, "I'm not a heavy-handed boss like those before me were and I work in a more collaborative, inclusive way without asserting my opinion first." (Judie Panneton, "Queen Anne, Sacramento's Anne Rudin ambitiously embraces retirement," *The Sacramento Bee, Discover Magazine,* Spring 1999).

"Rudin said while women are judged and held to a higher standard than their male counterparts, 'they don't have to model themselves after a man and they need to be comfortable with their own style of leadership'" (Panneton). When Anne first joined the Council in

1971, those serving on the Council were commonly referred to as the "city fathers." As the sole woman, Anne was viewed as an outsider by the men sitting at the dais with her. Gradually, through hard work and persistence (which did not include making coffee), Anne began to be accepted and respected by her colleagues. But they were uncomfortable. After all, this was to a large extent still the era of the "company man," when men dominated government, business, the arts, charitable organizations, social clubs, etc. And their dominance was protected by the organizations themselves, which were often hierarchical in nature and rewarded adherence to a military style chain of command. The goal or vision of the organization was all-important, so the means of achieving the goal was far less important than the prize. Information was viewed as a valuable commodity, guarded by the men at the top and doled out to underlings on an as-needed basis. Leaders often believed that they should motivate their employees with fear and keep them off balance and in constant competition; that the end product or profit would be better as a result. Collaboration was viewed by some with suspicion.

In the '70s, women were starting to enter the workforce in greater numbers, but few were reaching the top levels of their chosen professions. They sought advice on how to beat the odds and move up in their organizations. Popular magazines published articles for women on how to succeed, saying: just be more like men.

Books about power-and-how-to-get-it, mostly written by men, assumed that women were not equipped to lead as women, and advised ambitious women to simply act like a man. In some ways it made sense. Male managers tended to engage in a cloning style of hiring and promoting men in their organizations. The men at the top identified with, encouraged, and mentored men just like them: White men who looked and thought just like them. If the men in power could just overlook gender and reward the behaviors of women acting like men, advancement by women might just be possible.

Academic studies about how women lead began to be published in the '80s and '90s. One such book, *The Female Advantage—Women's Ways of Leadership*, by Sally Helgesen, came out in 1990. To understand what male managers actually did, Helgesen relied, in part, on the research of management scientist Henry Mintzberg. To assemble the hard data of an empirical study, Mintzberg followed five male managers through their workdays and kept a minute by minute diary of their activities, even the most mundane tasks. This allowed him to avoid generalizations and pinpoint what managers were doing well and not so well. Mintzberg's 1968 Ph.D dissertation became the basis for his 1973 book, *The Nature of Managerial Work*. Mintzberg observed that the men at the top of their organizations identified themselves with their positions. The existence of wives and children was extraneous, and intrusions by family into work life were unwelcome. Information was their chief source of power and it was hoarded. Unscheduled tasks and encounters were seen as annoying interruptions to the flow of work. Thus, a role of secretaries was to protect their bosses from unwanted intrusions.

Helgesen's analysis of ways women work and lead also relied on a minute by minute diary of the activities of four women. There were some similarities—top female and male leaders spent 20% to 40% of their time with clients, peers or colleagues, and both female and male leaders felt that a major aspect of their jobs was to represent their organizations in the greater world—but beyond that, Helgesen observed few similarities in how women and men led. Helgesen's central conclusion about female leadership was that women lead by networking. Rather than employing a top-down leadership style like men, successful women leaders placed themselves at the center of a web of relationships that encouraged the flow of information. Rather than hoard information, women scheduled time to share information, which they saw as a two-way street. Unlike the company men of Mintzberg's study, the women leaders in Helgesen's observations saw themselves as multi-faceted with complex identities. This was in part due to their roles as mothers. One leader explained, "Having a baby gives you a sense of what's really important. You still work like hell, but it's all in perspective."

Women also tended to see the big picture, while men were inclined to become overly involved in the day-to-day tasks of management, depriving them of the time to contemplate the big picture. Whereas men did not welcome interruptions to their work, women liked live action encounters and welcomed activities not directly related to their work. They also made time to keep lines of communication open by thoughtfully responding to mail and phone calls. Notably, women viewed their decisions in light of the likely impacts on society generally, including effects on the family, education, the environment, even world peace.

Although Helgesen's study was published nearly 20 years after Anne Rudin first held office, Anne was acutely aware of the differences in leadership by men and women. She did not try to copy the men with whom she served. She celebrated her multi-faceted role as mother, wife, and community leader. She welcomed young women and girls to her office, giving them Susan B. Anthony silver dollars as an inspirational gesture. When she was elected Mayor in 1983, she invited women artist friends to loan her artwork to be displayed in her office. Anne Rudin is admired for her many accomplishments in support of a better environment, public health through smoking cessation, advancement of the arts, including the Sacramento Symphony, campaign finance reform, light rail development, and support of gay rights.

But Rudin also had a larger view of her role as city council member and mayor. She used the influence of her office to fight for nuclear disarmament, the banning of assault weapons, and to promote bilateral relationships between Japan and the United States. In 2005, the Japanese Ministry of Foreign Affairs awarded Rudin the Foreign Ministries Commendation. And in 2018, the Boat Pond in William

Photo courtesy of Sacramento League of Women Voters

Councilmembers Lyla Ferris and Heather Fargo, Mayor Anne Rudin and Councilmember Lynn Robie (L to R) at the Sacramento LWV State of the Community luncheon honoring retiring Mayor Anne Rudin, 1992

Land Park was renamed the Mayor Anne Rudin Peace Pond and graced with a commemorative sign to honor Anne's long-time support for the Japanese American community locally, and the Japanese reparations movement more generally.

Fierce Advocates

Councilwoman Lyla Ferris, elected to represent District 2 in 1987, was a fierce advocate for her community, which was historically underserved as compared to the wealthier neighborhoods of the city. She set out to level the playing field by understanding and influencing the budget process, especially the Capital Improvements Projects budget:

> My highest priority when I was elected was to get badly needed infrastructure improvements in my district. I thought it was shameful that Robla, roughly a third of my district, did not have city sewer services and could not get city sewer services. The capacity was not there, staff told me. There is no slope left, they said. So, I asked, how do we get more slope? It will take lots of money and installation of a

major new sewer main, was the response. The staff knew it was badly needed, but there had never been anyone to really advocate for the Robla area. I was the first council member elected who had lived for 25 years in Robla. I knew the problems there. I had to let my colleagues know what was needed. By the time Heather [Fargo] was elected two years later, I had secured the funding necessary for the sewer main extension to finally bring city sewer service to that area.

Ferris noted that "women have a different way of looking at problems." Her successful advocacy for basic services in the Robla area impressed newcomer to the council, Heather Fargo, and they became allies and fast friends.

Deborah Ortiz was elected to represent District 5 in a special election in March 1993 (to replace Joe Serna when he was elected mayor). Like Lyla Ferris, Deborah came from a historically underserved area, Oak Park. Her election represented a milestone: the first popularly elected Latina in Sacramento history. (Eva Garcia was appointed in 1983 to complete Lloyd Connelly's unexpired term after he was elected to the State Assembly, but Garcia decided not to run for election to the District 6 seat.)

Ortiz represented a younger generation than the trailblazing women born and raised during the Depression. But, like Illa Collin, Lynn Robie, and Kay Knepprath, Ortiz was no stranger to poverty and discrimination. In the 1930s, her grandparents came to Sacramento, where her grandfather worked as a farm worker contractor. Her mother only completed the ninth grade, becoming pregnant at age 16 and mothering five children by the time she was 21 (four boys and one girl, Deborah, born in 1957). By age 31, her mother was divorced and the family was living on public assistance. Adamant that Deborah not get pregnant, her mother insisted that her daughter must do well in school and set her sights high. Ortiz did, graduating from McClatchy High School, U.C. Davis, and McGeorge School of Law before working in State government and running for City Council in 1993.

Prior to running for City Council, Ortiz served on the Oak Park Project Area Committee, the U.C. Davis Medical Center Community Advisory Board, the City Planning Commission, and on the City Redistricting Commission representing the Latino Coalition for Fair Sacramento Redistricting.

As mayor, Heather Fargo served the city as a whole. When asked whether she had a clear set of goals when she took office in 2001, she explained:

> Yes, I had an agenda, but being Mayor is a lot like traveling. You have to deal with what goes wrong. You lose your luggage. You've got to get your luggage back. Things happen. I was mayor when we had 9/11. I was supposed to have lunch with my dad that day.... It was his birthday....That didn't happen. I got picked up by a police officer and the City Manager. We went to the airport. We had a press conference.

Regular unexpected crises changed the course of other well-planned days. Public outrage over such things as the police shooting of an unarmed young black man or scandalous sexual misconduct by city fire fighters on one Fourth of July had a habit of changing the narrative.

The Power of No

While Heather Fargo is justifiably proud of her many accomplishments as a community activist, City Councilmember and Mayor, she also commented on the power of saying "No." When a prominent and influential developer was turned down on his proposed high rise office building at 16th and R streets, that "no" effectively saved the R Street Master Plan, one that had been carefully hammered out by a coalition of wide ranging interests. Heather said, "That site is now housing and retail, as envisioned by the plan. The rest of R St. has been going through a revival...."

Another "no" resulted in saving the Bellevue Apartments at 8th and L streets, as well as a long-time Chinese restaurant at ground level. In August 2019, the apartment house reopened with 24 refurbished affordable housing units—a big win for affordable housing in Sacramento.

Heather's audacious bluff while discussing a developer's proposal to replace sycamore trees around the Federal Courthouse with palm trees resulted in retaining the many sycamores that provide shade to the over 1 million people a year who use the Amtrak station. "I said no even though I had no authority to do so."

The unremitting thirst for water by the East Bay Municipal Utility District (EBMUD) resulted in their request to divert water from the American River to the Sacramento River, a request met with another firm "No." Even though EBMUD lost a 17-year lawsuit to take water from the American River, "they asked again for a water intake further up the American River and were again told no," recalled Heather, "when we were told they would need to dig up the length of Sacramento for a pipe. We eventually got them to build the intake just south of the Pocket area along the Sacramento River."

The Power of Thank You

Another distinctive trait in women who hold power is that women tend not to dominate, boast, or bully. Soon after joining the City Council (District 8) in 1979, Lynn Robie realized that her new job as part-time City Council representative could not be done well without the help of the city's professional staff, who graciously helped her sort out the very complex issues facing the city. Staff also accompanied her to some highly contentious neighborhood meetings. Robie recalled:

> It had been a very long time since an elected representative had visited historically underserved neighborhoods such as Meadowview. They

were justifiably angry and really let me have it for my first year in office. Gradually I built trust with neighborhood leaders and we were able to get things done.

After relying on staff expertise at such meetings, Lynn made a point of thanking them and praising their performance.

A Unified Bloc?

Many of the women who ran for local office and worked to support and elect one another became fast friends, looking after each other's children, celebrating the marriage of their children, and welcoming grandchildren into the world. Likewise, the friendship formed by Sandra Smoley and Muriel Johnson in 1958 in the Midwest, where their husbands were finishing up their medical studies, lasted decades. Beyond being friends and kindred spirits, did this group of elected women consistently stand together as a female bloc or in unity over issues of conscience?

According to Kim Mueller, there was only one issue during the four years she served on the Council where the women formed a bloc against the men. That issue was whether and to what extent Sacramento voters should subsidize another professional sports team, the Oakland Raiders NFL football team. Between 1987 and 1990, the Raiders were shopping for the best public subsidy they could get, pitting one city against the other after a failed venture in Los Angeles. In 1990, the Sacramento City Council unanimously agreed to give Al Davis, the owner of the team, $50 million for the NFL franchise fee to move to Sacramento, but Davis was slow to put his money where his mouth was. The men on the Council were smitten, but the five women on the Council knew the guys were being played to maximum advantage and sought to hold the Raiders' feet to the fire. After the women teamed up to set a clear deadline for Davis to commit to Sacramento and he failed to do so, the brief affair with the Raiders ended.

Councilmember Lauren Hammond recalled that in 2006 there were four women on the City Council and, while they didn't form a unified front on most issues, they operated differently from their male colleagues. "Women really do weave webs," recalled Hammond, who credited Illa Collin for being her mentor and encouraging her to enter local government. Collin appointed Hammond to the County Planning Commission, where Lauren became grounded in land use planning and the ways local government impacts citizens' lives.

While the women on the Council often shared a humanistic world view and advanced proposals to address social injustice, correct gender inequality, improve the environment, and foster the arts, when it came down to the day-to-day issues that were important to their constituents, they focused first and foremost on voter concerns and the delivery of basic services such as modern sewer lines, safe drinking water, street lights, stop signs and traffic lights, parks, community centers, and libraries. For most women, elected office was primarily about serving their fellow citizens and less about amassing power and climbing the political ladder.

But there was occasional tension between principle and process among council members. In 1990, the United States military was fighting the Gulf War against Iraq and a fervor for visible patriotism was running high. In a bid to re-introduce the Pledge of Allegiance at the start of each City Council meeting, two female pacifists, Mayor Anne Rudin and Councilwoman Kim Mueller, approached the question differently. Rudin was a firm "no" for reasons of principle. Mueller, who represented a blue-collar district that was both patriotic and tolerant, joined the majority and voted "yes." Rudin, somewhat miffed at Mueller, pointedly invited Kim to lead the audience in the Pledge of Allegiance at the next Council meeting.

A Slice of Time

In the years since Sacramento first began electing Council members by district, the modestly paid position has evolved from being a part-time job with one secretary shared by eight Council members, to a very demanding full time commitment. In addition to interacting with constituents and addressing their concerns, elected officials at both the City and County level must read and sort through very complex matters of law, policy, and budget. Regular meetings of the City Council and Board of Supervisors are the most visible to the public, but local elected representatives must also serve on a vast array of other official committees, boards, and commissions.

Lauren Hammond, first elected in 1997 and the first Black woman ever to be elected to the Council, faced an endurance test upon taking her oath of office: she was assigned to at least nine Joint Powers Authorities (JPA's) that set policy and made recommendations regarding

Councilmember Lauren Hammond, 2004.

public transit, solid waste management, employment training, air quality management, the library system, regional sanitation, and local and regional government. Hammond also met regularly with the business associations for Downtown, Franklin Blvd., Oak Park, and Stockton Blvd. Since the City Council sits simultaneously as the Housing and Redevelopment Authority (SHRA), she mastered those complex issues and regulations. In addition, Hammond chaired the City's Employment and Appointments Committee, followed by the Law and Legislation Committee. "These meetings were both daytime and evening. Any given week I had three outside board meetings and two Council meetings per week. Over the weekend there were neighborhood events to attend." She recalled:

I had town hall meetings in every neighborhood of my district. All the neighbors wanted their area to look better. The business owners wanted more customers and an inviting street. We found money to landscape empty lots, clean up illegal dumping, and fund boulevard improvements for every major street in the district including Florin Road, 24th Street, Franklin Blvd., Freeport Blvd., Broadway, and Stockton Blvd.

Typically, every day Monday through Friday I had appointments with City staff, developers, staff from JPA's, activists, constituents, etc. Every Monday we had a staff meeting to help prioritize the workload. I was told by my predecessor that Council District 5 had a high volume of constituent calls and requests for service. That never changed. We also got requests from residents from other districts as well. The late Mayor Joe Serna said only the mayor's office gets more calls. He was right. And no subsequent mayor disagreed.

Once I tried to count the actual hours per week I worked. I stopped counting at 60 hours. It was probably closer to 80. My staff also worked more than 40 hours per week.

My goal as a new Councilmember was to open teen resource centers citywide. We were finally able to create the Office of Youth Development after the '90s recession but it was cut with the 2006 recession and recovery.

I noticed Oak Park had a disproportionate number of renters with out-of-town landlords. I worked with SHRA and community groups to encourage home ownership. We created a study group of bankers, developers, SHRA, urban planners, and other stakeholders. Together we wrote the Oak Park Renaissance Project. The goal was to take that portion of the neighborhood with the most empty lots and abandoned homes and get small developers to build houses there.

Supervisor Illa Collin's service to the community was strategically focused on the environment, neighborhoods, social programs for children and the elderly, homelessness, mental illness, and poverty. Like Hammond, Collin's time was largely taken up by meetings.

Here is a look at how Collin and her colleagues on the Board typically spent their time while performing official duties: Regularly scheduled meetings of the Board of Supervisors were held on Tuesdays and Wednesdays, generally from 9 a.m. to noon, then back at 2 p.m. to reume the session. Tuesdays were mostly concerned with official County business, while Wednesdays were focused on planning issues. Prior to the meetings, Illa often met with constituents, County staff, and developers. In addition to preparing for and attending the regular meetings of the Board, Illa Collin represented the Board of Supervisors on the following bodies during her 28 years in office:

- SETA (Sacramento Employment & Training Agency, a joint powers agency which administers employment programs, Head Start programs, community action, and refugee assistance monies

- LAFCO (Local Agency Formation Commission) which makes decisions relating to annexation and incorporations

- Sacramento Metropolitan Cable Television Commission, a joint powers agency which monitors and regulates the cable television franchise

- Adult Facilities Detention Committee, which focuses on the intake and operational elements of the entire County adult prison system

- Juvenile Justice System Task Force

- Children's Agenda

- Sacramento Regional Transit District Board of Directors, which operates the public transportation system of buses and light rail in the Sacramento area

- City Transportation and Community Development Committee & SMUD's Planning Committee

- Downtown Transportation Task Force (alternate)

- Los Angeles/Fresno/Bay Area/Sacramento High Speed Rail Corridor Committee
- Policy Advisory Committee (Interstate 80 Corridor)
- Steering Committee of the Caltrans Rail Task Force
- Sacramento Transportation Authority
- Sacramento Area Commerce and Trade Organization
- Sacramento Valley Air Basin Coordinating Council
- Multi-Disciplinary Interview Committee
- Sacramento City/County Library Authority

While official Board business was mostly conducted during the day, LAFCO, the Library Authority, and the Cable Commission met in the evenings. Although the long hours spent on official business might be a daunting prospect to some, Collin relished every minute in her role as Supervisor, especially meeting people and learning from them. Her enthusiasm didn't end with human interaction. Collin's administrative assistant, Joyce Mihanovich, chuckled as she recalled, "Illa probably went to every dog show in town."

CHAPTER SIX

Did I Sign Up for This?

You have incredible—and sometimes humiliating—experiences in public.
—Illa Collin

If Animals Could Vote

A *cow town.* That was what big city pundits in San Francisco and L.A. called Sacramento in the late 20th Century. Devoted Sacramentans were insulted by the label; however, they were hard put to counter it when a pig named Porky waddled in as a witness at a 1991 Sacramento City Council meeting. Porky was a family's 1990 Christmas gift, a 26-pound pot-bellied Vietnamese pig, a pet who strolled through Alkali Flat on a leash and was loved by mom, dad, and their three children, ages 4, 6, and 8. However, livestock had been outlawed in the city of Sacramento since 1879. A *Bee* writer, in a moment of whimsy, wrote that "trouble came when someone squealed and then it became apparent that Porky's bacon was on the line." Despite Porky being a pet, "to Sacramento City Hall, a pig is a pig, plain and simple." The ordinance against farm animals in the city required that Porky be banished. His family wanted an exception.

Anne Rudin was mayor and there were four other women on the Council (Fargo, Ferris, Mueller, Robie) when Porky, a District 1 constituent of Councilwoman Fargo, clicked his toes into the Council chambers, trailing an entourage of delighted media. Ultimately, the Council voted eight to one in Porky's favor, allowing the city to license miniature pigs, and Porky received the first license.

The issue was happily resolved. It's easy to picture the Council exiting City Hall smiling and thinking that their deliberations about animals in the City were over. They didn't know about the comfort duck then, of course.

"Andora," Heather Fargo recalled, then grinned. "Leave it to me to remember the duck's name and not the girl's."

Andora faced the same problem as Porky: she was a farm animal—a white Muscovy duck with a black halo on her head. Her owner's situation, however, was very serious. A 20-year-old paraplegic, Deborah Denbaugh, was given the duck as an Easter gift in 1992. According to *The Sacramento Bee*, Deborah, "who has an unknown seizure disorder and has suffered from quadriplegia since age 16, didn't respond to any of the therapies her doctors offered … With the duck, named Andora, as her bedside companion, Denbaugh began to move and speak … improvements that stunned her mother and friends."

Mayor Anne Rudin announced from the outset that the Council seemed to approve of the woman keeping her duck, with proper documentation of its service. The problem was, someone had complained, and the City's chief animal control officer advised, "We have to respond when we receive a complaint" (John Howard, *Associated Press*). As in Porky's case, the animal won. Andora went home with her human. The law was subsequently changed to automatically exempt documented "therapeutic animals."

Unusual issues continued to descend upon the City Council. In August 1991, arguments were brought on behalf of employees forced to work outdoors for longer than eight hours, sometimes in heat above 100 degrees, and frequently without breaks. Unthinkable! At least according to the Society for the Prevention of Cruelty to Animals, advocates for the horses that pulled tourist carriages around Old Sacramento.

The Council was the judge for the horses' workplace issues. Owners of the carriage companies argued that proposed regulations were too strict; the SPCA argued they were too lax. The result? According to *The Sacramento Bee*: "The horses no longer will be allowed to work when temperatures top 100 degrees and the animals will be required to take a 20-minute break after two hours' work and a half-hour break after both four and six hours' work." None could work more than eight hours a day ("Rules Aid").

Not all animal interactions that City leaders had to deal with came before the Council. Heather Fargo shared the story of a hummingbird:

> I was mayor then and, you know, had been so involved with animal care. It was the end of the day and I was going to my car–planned to visit my mom, I remember–when this guy came up to me. He held out his hand and there was a hummingbird. He said it needed help and gave it to me. There were little kids around right then. 'Oh, can we see?' they said. So I let the little kids see the hummingbird. I took it to animal care, and they said they would give it some sugar water and see what they could do. I left it there and drove to see my mom. Next day I got a call from the director of animal care. He said, 'I just wanted to let you know the hummingbird was revived and we let it go this morning and all is fine.'

She grinned. "A mayor's work."

A serious Council discussion turned pointed when the City Council weighed Sacramento's own vulnerability to flooding following Hurricane Katrina in New Orleans. The levee break that allowed flood waters to inundate New Orleans prompted the City Council to worry about their own vulnerable levee system and the people and animals in need of rescue in the event of a flood. The issue was that rescuers in New Orleans left family pets behind. Heather Fargo, a strong animal lover, was appalled that family pets were abandoned and urged adoption of a more humane animal rescue policy in Sacramento. Naysayers argued against such a policy, citing limited space in rescue transport vehicles. "Think about it," chided Heather to a male Council colleague, "Do you want your wife to have to choose between you and your dog?" The Council adopted a more humane policy.

Mayor Fargo also led efforts to improve conditions at Sacramento's Animal Shelter. Given Heather's many interactions with and on behalf of our furry and flying friends, it came as no surprise to hear her quip, "If animals could vote, I'd still be mayor."

The Sewer Viewer Furor

In 1990, for the first time (and so far, the *only* time), more than half the nine-member Sacramento City Council was female. The Public Works Department noted the female ascendancy and, sort of tongue-in-cheek, suggested a competition, introduced with the bureaucratic label, "Manhole Terminology Change Contest." Its purpose? To rename those round, cast iron covers on the openings into Sacramento's sewer system referred to at that time as manhole covers. There were 26,379 of them, after all.

The four councilwomen and the mayor were amused by the change but had not requested it and were shocked when something about the renaming triggered worldwide attention. Long before social media or instantly-transmitted images, the issue of renaming manhole covers went viral. In the Associated Press at the time, John Howard reported, "Responses—much to the astonishment of city officials—have come in from all over the world. . . . One newspaper headline said the city was 'Blowing the lid off sexist manholes,' while another proclaimed that a 'Tempest in a manhole sweeps city.'" A radio station in one of Sacramento's sister cities, Hamilton, New Zealand, held a contest for its citizens to suggest new names. Suggestions included "people hole," "peephole," and "underground service access (USA) hole." The winner? "Sewer viewer."

Howard quoted a Sacramento city receptionist who revealed, "Many people are calling with 'lewd and offensive suggestions,' and others angrily want to know about 'the women who are taking over the City Council.'" A representative of the National Organization of

Women defended, "If you suggest a change, immediately there is the uproar, people saying, 'Oh, those women. There they go again.' Some people are threatened by something as simple as changing the names of manhole covers" (Howard).

Unperturbed by the wide publicity, Sacramento leaders largely ignored the issue. Its resolution came indirectly. In a report that came before the Council, the "manhole covers" were referred to as "maintenance covers." Since "manhole cover" and "maintenance cover" could each be identified on city utility maps by "MC," the maps would require no change if *maintenance* were adopted. Quietly, without fanfare, the report was approved. "Maintenance covers" the lids became and remain to this day.

Despite the somewhat frivolous international take on the subject, the reality is that words *do* have power. Use of "man" implies that the employee is male. This time, use of the word man as the generic was dropped (into the sewer, one presumes).

You Want Me to Do What?

The challenges of being a celebrity guest also made their way into the women's shared memories. Donkey basketball was what got to Illa Collin. "It was my short legs," she complained after a charity donkey basketball game. Bill Lindelof of *The Sacramento Bee* compiled a few of Illa's reflections as she neared retirement and explained, "Her short legs, compared with fellow competitor and current Supervisor Don Nottoli—made getting on and off her steed a bit difficult."

Collin wasn't all that thrilled with the Folsom soapbox derby race down a steep hill either. "I didn't know how to steer it, and there was no braking," she said. City Councilmember Sandy Sheedy chuckled in memory of wheelchair basketball with Bonnie Pannell, neither of whom had maneuvering skills: "It was hilarious!"

Even more adventurous was the ride on the submarine that was "surface cruising" its way up the Sacramento Deep Water Channel to what is now the Port of West Sacramento. Supervisor Collin and Mayor Rudin were invited to take a ride. Collin told Lindelof, "What we didn't know was that the captain was so nervous about bringing the submarine to the ship channel, that he wasn't stopping that submarine for anything. So Anne and I had to leap from a moving boat to the submarine." They both landed safely, although Illa expressed thanks to "helping hands grabbing us." Harrowing as it may have been at the time, as it aged into memory, it made a great story.

Mayor Rudin and Supervisor Collin traveled to one of Sacramento's sister cities. Collin recalled, "We were told not to drink the water in China, so we drank all this beer." Not an easy task for two women who rarely drank. The guests were treated with the utmost courtesy. Mayor Rudin was offered the honor of sitting in a throne-like chair. It was, their Chinese hosts said with pride, where President Richard Nixon sat. Collin said, "Anne didn't want to look at us, but she gave me that look like, don't you dare come near laughing."

Photo courtesy of Anne Rudin Family Collection

Supervisor Illa Collin and Mayor Anne Rudin in Jinan, China, a Sacramento Sister City, 1991

Evidently their hosts didn't know that Rudin and Collin were staunch Democrats.

Fun on the Council

It wasn't all serious hard work on the Council. In 1995, Halloween fell on Tuesday when the Council met. The proper attire? Well, a witch's hat at the least, which the women wore. Just remembering events, Heather Fargo's story started Lyla Ferris laughing. Then Fargo caught the giggles. She admitted, "I would get Lyla laughing when we were on the Council. She sat next to me. Then Anne would give us The Look. One day Anne told me, 'You know, you're part of the trouble.'" Lyla remembered fellow Councilmember Josh Pane, a fellow light spirit. Heather recalled, "Anne would get mad at him because he would do such funny things. She would say things to him in Italian."

Less direct, but equally on point, was a discussion about the number of women's restrooms that should be in the Sacramento Convention Center theater being rebuilt at that time. When the convention center manager did not heed Fargo's argument that more women's restrooms were needed, she called his wife for assistance. "He came in the next day pointing his finger at me," she laughed. "'That's cheating!' he said. But we got the extra bathrooms."

Photo by Larry Dalton

Councilmember Sandy Sheedy, 2004

Sandy Sheedy recounted the biker dispute. A burly fellow wearing the requisite leathers testified before the Council, followed by a burly woman who looked directly at Sheedy and challenged, "Did he scare you?" Sheedy, in her most silken voice, replied, "No, I'm not afraid of you. I've always liked Harley men." Meanwhile, Councilmember Bonnie Pannell was shaking her head, unable to contain her laughter. Recalling her twelve years on the Council, Pannell said, "We had fun. We were a close knit group."

Part Two

Defining Sacramento

Big League City, Camellia Capital, City of Trees, Farm to Fork Capital, River City, State Capital, Cow Town, the Big Tomato, that valley town located halfway between San Francisco and Lake Tahoe. Regardless of the slogans or slurs applied to Sacramento, it is the turning points that best define what and who we are. Some of Sacramento's turning points came in response to threats to our health, heritage, or environment. Other changes in direction have come about as a result of an abiding belief that our community can do and be better.

Part Two of *We Can Do This!* focuses on the defining moments and sustained efforts led by women to make Sacramento a welcoming and beautiful community.

The American River Parkway

The ubiquitous sounds of suburban America—automobiles, lawn mowers, backhoes, and sirens—are mostly unheard on the 31 miles of Sacramento's urban parkway. Instead, the melodic sound of river rapids mingled with birdsong provides a calming escape from supercharged modern life. A float down the river in a raft provides a visual calmness as well. Oaks, cottonwoods, wild grasses, great blue herons, and the occasional angler dot the shore. Relatively few trophy mansions intrude on the scene.

The visionaries who imagined a wilderness escape in the midst of urban Sacramento—the nationally recognized American River Parkway—saw the potential as early as 1915, but it took the combined efforts of professional park planners, dedicated citizens, and elected officials to achieve the reality we have today in the form of a scenic parkway stretching from the confluence of the Sacramento and American Rivers to Folsom Lake. Over one hundred years after Sacramento city planner John Nolen first floated the idea, the parkway attracts about 8 million visitors annually, including people in boats, on foot, on horses, and on bicycles. Not just a local recreational resource, annual use of the parkway "exceeds the annual attendance at every federal and state park in California except the Golden Gate Recreational Area" (Peter J. Hayes, *The Lower American River Prehistory to Parkway*).

While the parkway concept has been generally accepted by the public from its inception, it has taken diligence to achieve legal status, fund land acquisition, and fend off intrusions. Tentative plans by the City, County, and Chamber of Commerce to beautify and develop recreational areas on both the Sacramento and American Rivers were drawn up in 1949. In 1959, the Board of Supervisors adopted an ordinance creating a County Department of Parks and Recreation, and planning for a county-wide park system began.

One trailblazing woman who saw the potential and challenge of assembling land for the initial 23-mile parkway was Effie Yeaw, a teacher and naturalist. She recognized that post-war suburban expansion during the 1950s was a real threat to the proposed parkway. In 1961, the County Planning Commission approved development plans for a subdivision within 125 feet of the river. "This was the act that rallied parkway forces. Within a few days a small group of civic leaders and representatives of conservation and youth groups met to lay the groundwork for the Save the American River Association (SARA). SARA speakers covered the community, recruited members, distributed pamphlets, and prepared a film." They "rallied the support necessary to convince the supervisors that the community was behind the preservation of the river and its bordering wild lands. In January 1962, the board officially adopted the Parkway plan and committed more funds for acquisition" (Hayes).

As a founder and charter member of SARA, Effie Yeaw urged acquisition of the first 70 acres of open space along the American River in Carmichael, part of the Deterding ranch, where she had spent years teaching school children about the natural world. In 1962, the Sacramento County Department of Parks and Recreation bought the land, successfully competing against a developer intent on subdividing the land for housing.

Also an early visionary for protecting and planting trees, Effie Yeaw won adoption of a County ordinance in 1957 to protect heritage oaks in Sacramento. The ordinance included: "a hearing by a committee of experts and other citizens before a tree could be removed; give special protection to large heritage trees; require private developers to provide trees removed during construction, and then maintain the replacements; and require public agencies to prevent destruction of oaks when street-widening or other projects threaten the trees" (Frederick R. Gunsky, *Effie Yeaw—Teacher, Naturalist, Visionary*).

Like most of the women who rose to the occasion of public service through advocacy in the '60s, '70s and '80s, Effie Yeaw was determined, persistent, and well-informed. She was described as "a gentle, lovely lady. But she was so competent they couldn't argue. She had the answers from the technical people. Nothing would stop her." (Gunsky) Although Effie Yeaw died in 1970, the organization she co-founded, SARA, and its allies have continually aroused public interest and worked to keep the county and city leaders faithful to the original vision of the American River Parkway. Effie Yeaw is memorialized with the Nature Center that welcomes visitors, especially school children, to the first piece of land acquired for the Parkway.

Another important link in the chain of visionary women who recognized and celebrated Sacramento's unique attributes was Jo Smith, who illustrated natural history books and instructional materials for Effie Yeaw and illustrated the campaign literature of many of the women covered in this book. Like Virginia Moose, who served as treasurer for the campaigns of Anne Rudin, Lynn Robie, Illa Collin, and Heather Fargo, Jo Smith was a solid and sustaining presence. In an era when pen to paper brought a human touch to a world without the internet or social media, Jo created fundraising invitations that conveyed the humanity, accessibility, and sense of humor of the first wave of women who began running for elective office in 1971.

A staunch supporter of the American River Parkway, Supervisor Illa Collin recalled,

> When I first moved here (1968), there was still gravel mining going on in the Parkway, and there were a lot of other activities going on as well. Because of that (1972) bond effort and because of the efforts of countless citizens, the Parkway was saved for future generations. (Hayes)

Vigilance to protect the American River Parkway from urbanization was a concern for Supervisor Collin when she retired in 2007. When she first took office in 1979, public support to preserve the region's riparian gem was strong and vocal, but the Board of Supervisors' resolve has been gradually eroded by pressure from development interests.

One such clash of private development rights versus zoning rules designed to reduce visual intrusion into the parkway involved 4.5 acres of grassland on Fair Oaks Bluff, towering 140 feet above the river—with million dollar trophy views of the river, Mount Diablo, and the Sierras. After the bluff was earmarked for development, outraged citizens formed a citizens group, led by American River College teacher Tracy Martin Shearer and assisted by the Sacramento Valley Conservancy, that "raised over $1 million to acquire half the property and turn it over to the County in 2003 for inclusion in the American River Parkway. The Fair Oaks Recreation and Park District signed for a bank loan obtained by the citizens' group on the remaining half as both groups held fundraising drives that secured the second half of the bluff" (Hayes). As she left office in 2007, Collin explained what concerned her most, and urged that "We must stop urbanization of the parkway—and by that I mean the monster houses you see, many approved on 3-2 vote." (Amy Yannello, *Sacramento News and Review*, Jan. 11, 2007).

Lauded by Sacramento Congresswoman Doris Matsui in the Congressional Record of January 24, 2007, Matsui noted,

> Supervisor Collin has consistently been praised for her environmental record and leadership. She helped create the Sacramento Tree Foundation and the American River Parkway Foundation (1983). She has received the Outstanding Service Award from the California Parks and Recreation Society as well as the Outstanding Public Official Award from the National Association of County Parks and Recreation officials. In 2005, Supervisor Collin received the Environmentalist of the Year Award from the Sacramento Chapter of the Sierra Club.

Thanks to the vision and perseverance of Sacramento's trailblazing women, residents and visitors to the region have numerous opportunities to access and enjoy the 31-mile American River Parkway, a true gem in our urban environment.

One Million Trees
Plant 1,000,000 trees. Ambitious, certainly. Less-idealistic types might have called it preposterous. But then, year by year, tree by tree, it has happened.

> —*The Sacramento Bee*, Editorial, May 1, 2001

Former Supervisor Illa Collin grew up on a treeless plain in Wyoming. She recalled that there were only two places where trees grew in her hometown of Rock Springs: the cemetery and around her house.

> I used to go to the cemetery every Decoration Day [as they called Memorial Day back then] and I would be amazed at the trees. My

mother had planted trees around our house trying to get them to grow, and we had little docks for them so the water from one would fall down to the other.

When Illa came to Sacramento in 1967, she was enthralled. "I saw the parks with all the trees, especially in Land Park which had all kinds of trees." She became a regular bike rider, cycling along city streets, awed by the green canopies under which she rode.

The Sacramento Tree Foundation's booklet, *Celebrating 25 Years*, describes what happened next:

> Always an advocate for trees, Illa Collin learned that the Board of Supervisors would be hearing the issue of cutting down heritage oak trees that graced Elk Grove Boulevard. Illa Collin knew these trees well from frequent bicycle trips from her home. She lobbied hard for the trees…but fell one vote short of saving the trees. The trees were cut down.
>
> Illa Collin decided that night she was going to run for County Supervisor. Never underestimate the power of a tree to create a candidate! Illa Collin won her bid for Supervisor in 1978 and she retired 30 years later in 2007. That same year (1978), the Sacramento County Public Works Department…cut down a number of trees on Auburn Boulevard. There was a huge public outcry against the 'butchering' of the trees, and newly-elected Supervisor Illa Collin responded with the creation of the Sacramento County Tree Task Force. (Jeanie Shaw, Eric Douglas, and Ray Tretheway, *Celebrating 25 Years*, Sacramento Tree Foundation, 2008)

Unfortunately for the Tree Task Force, California's Proposition 13 passed in 1978, bringing vast cuts to public funding. In financial crises, funding for trees has little priority against budgets for law enforcement and fire protection. The Tree Task Force plodded on, supporting passage of an oak tree preservation ordinance, then an ordinance that set county standards for parking lot shade (a similar bill was passed by the City later that year), but it was increasingly clear that some private funding was called for.

Supervisor Illa Collin and Sacramento Mayor Phil Isenberg took on this issue together. In 1981 they called a meeting of community activists to address the planting and stewardship of trees in our city and county. Settling on the idea of a private non-profit, they established a steering committee that included Illa Collin, Jane Hagedorn, Jean Runyon, Heather Fargo, and Linda Budge (Fargo and Budge both went on to be elected to local offices). Inviting 350 community leaders to their first meeting, they drew 150. Jane Hagedorn recalled, "We raised $17,000 in pledges. I was the first president of this group, called the Sacramento Tree Foundation [STF]."

As the Sacramento Tree Foundation learned early on, "It was one thing to plop trees into the ground beside Fair Oaks Boulevard and receive a lot of media coverage; it was another to keep the trees alive and thriving in this hot, asphalt-dominated environment" (Shaw). Executive Director Ray Tretheway recalled, "I remember that first summer, watering the 30 new trees on Fair Oaks Boulevard. I contrived two 50-gallon drums with a hose spigot, placed them in the back of my 1952 Dodge truck and twice a week hauled hoses from the drums to water the trees" (Shaw).

The Tree Foundation persevered, and by 1989 it was actively planting and caring for trees. Jeanie Shaw recalled the next step. On New Year's Eve 1989, she and Assemblyman Lloyd Connelly were at the home of Councilmember Kim Mueller. Mueller asked Jeanie and Lloyd to write down on a sketchpad a dream for the last decade of the millennium. Jeanie Shaw wrote, "Plant one million trees in Sacramento by the year 2000" (Shaw).

Mueller took up the challenge, calling on Illa Collin to be a co-sponsor. The effort was officially named "Trees for Tomorrow, a Gift to the 21st Century," and was co-chaired by Mueller, Collin,

Photo courtesy of Sacramento Tree Foundation

Tenth anniversary celebration of the Sacramento Tree Foundation. (L to R) Winston Ashizawa, Jane Hagedorn, Jeanie Shaw, former Mayor Phil Isenberg, Supervisor Illa Collin, Ray Tretheway, Ema Olsen, Judy Reyen.

and Shaw. Very quickly both the City Council and the Board of Supervisors endorsed the campaign and, in 1990, Trees for Tomorrow was given a place on the Sacramento Tree Foundation's executive committee.

On National Arbor Day in 2001, the Tree Foundation reached its goal. On a sunny Friday, the first of May, the millionth tree—a native valley oak— was planted in Cesar Chavez Park across from City Hall.

It is easy to take the world we live in for granted, as if what exists simply happened; but in fact, in Sacramento we move daily through a tree-shaded world built for us by far-sighted leaders, including Eleanor McClatchy, president of McClatchy Newspapers from 1936 to 1978 (publishers of *The Sacramento Bee)*, a fierce advocate for Sacramento's trees. Efforts continue to enlarge Sacramento's tree canopy, including tree plantings at schools with children helping, plantings in various communities, garden showcases and training programs, arboreal tours, and shade tree giveaways.

In 2011, still passionate about planting trees 34 years after her initial role in forming the Sacramento Tree Foundation (STF), Jane Hagedorn and other key Arden Park neighborhood leaders raised concerns with Supervisor Susan Peters about health and safety hazards caused by dead or dying Modesto ash trees in their community. With help from the County to remove ailing trees, 2,000 new trees—supplied by STF in partnership with the Sacramento Municipal Utility District (SMUD)—have been planted by Arden Park volunteers. Beginning with its $17,000 in pledges in 1992, STF now partners with SMUD to provide free deciduous trees that help lower electricity demand, reduce air pollution, manage storm-water runoff, and bring living, breathing beauty to our lives.

Today, if you check public lists of cities around the world with the most trees per capita, you will find Sacramento in almost every group's Top Ten. We live in a lush, green city where driving under tree-limb arches is a daily experience. We enjoy such greenery in our city because late in the last century, dedicated people such as Effie Yeaw, Illa Collin, Kim Mueller, Jane Hagedorn, and Heather Fargo planted the seeds—or at least the seedlings—to bring about our urban forest.

The Fight for Clean Air

Like most of the women who rose to leadership positions in Sacramento in the '70s, '80s and '90s, Jane Hagedorn was not a native, arriving as a newcomer in 1971. Born in Virginia and raised in Ohio, Jane came from a traditionally conservative family that valued hard work and fiscal restraint yet understood the importance of environmental stewardship and protecting public health.

Photo courtesy of Sacramento Tree Foundation

Jane Hagedorn, CEO of Breathe California of Sacramento- Emigrant Trails, 2006 (formerly American Lung Association of Sacramento-Emigrant Trails)

Hagedorn noticed that, while her adopted home was a wonderful place to raise her two children, threats to the quality of life in the state capital were beginning to spiral out of control. Rapid, unrestrained suburban growth meant the loss of prime agricultural land, and the unremitting construction of freeways clogged with smog-producing traffic triggered a steady rise in lung-related diseases.

In the 1970s, the environmental movement was just beginning to flex its muscles nationally, in California, and in Sacramento. When Hagedorn learned that a new umbrella organization (a group of groups) was being contemplated to address Sacramento's environmental challenges, she volunteered to help and quickly demonstrated her organizational savvy and capacity for hard work. As a part-time volunteer at the American Lung Association of Sacramento-Emigrant Trails (ALASET), she helped bring together the Lung Association, the American Association of University Women (AAUW), the League of Women Voters (LWV), the Sierra Club, the Audubon Society, the Ecology Information Center, and the Medical Society in 1971 to form the Environmental Council of Sacramento (ECOS).

Smoke Gets in Your Eyes

In the '70s, Sacramento residents had grudgingly come to accept the haze of brown smoke generated by burning rice stubble in the fall. But the growing evidence of severe health effects from the particulate matter in such seasonal smoke persuaded key groups to address the problem. Now Executive Director of the Lung Association, Jane Hagedorn brought together stakeholders such as farmers, environmentalists, physicians, city residents, and researchers from U.C. Davis and asked them to develop policy positions and look for alternatives to burning. Unable to find a local solution to a regional problem, the State Air Resources Board was consulted in the early '80s, and the agency agreed to manage a burn program that spread burning throughout the year, not just in the fall. While this reduced concentrated burning, it did not eliminate the health hazard. Finally, in 1991, with the leadership and co-sponsorship of Assemblyman Lloyd Connelly (member of the Sacramento City Council from 1976 to 1982), a state law to phase out rice stubble burning was passed. The goal of the Rice Straw Burning Reduction Act of 1991 was to reduce burning and eliminate it by the year 2000. While rice burning was not totally eliminated, it was reduced to about half of the valley's rice fields. According to the California Rice Growers Association, between 1980 and 2010 pollutants were reduced 80 to 90 percent.

Taking on Big Tobacco

When Jane Hagedorn joined the American Lung Association of Sacramento-Emigrant Trails in the early '70s, there was no better poster child for evil than the American tobacco industry. At that time, the tobacco industry needed to addict 3,500 people a day in order to replace the number of men and women who either kicked the habit or died each day. Jane explained that "since 60% of all people who smoke started by age 14, and 90% by age 20, this means the industry's primary target is children." After Congress banned airing cigarette ads on TV and radio in 1970, big tobacco turned to print advertising with a vengeance, targeting young aspirational women. One 1984 cooking magazine, *Cuisine*, contained seven full-page color advertisements for cigarettes, with two equating female success with smoking; one stated "You've come a long way, baby."

Jane recalled that the powerful lobbyists of big tobacco took note in 1974, when the Lung Association was able to convince the Sacramento City Council and County Board of Supervisors to prohibit smoking in retail stores and public meetings. Jane recalled, "From then on it became a deadly struggle between us and the tobacco interests. The stakes were high because Sacramento is the capital city of the biggest state in the Union. We are a major media market, and anti-smoking activists were becoming too successful."

When Jane Hagedorn, Assemblyman Lloyd Connelly, Deputy Director of the Lung Association Curt Mekemson, and Jerry Meral of the Planning and Conservation League proposed raising the state's cigarette tax from 10 cents to 25 cents per pack in 1986, they kicked off the biggest political fight of their lives. The proposed tax increase was earmarked for anti-smoking and research efforts. Using an organizing technique she had applied in her previous campaigns to save native oaks in California, Jane formed a statewide coalition of 19 other lung associations and community and health groups to build grassroots support for proposed legislation for raising the cigarette tax. When the bill came up for a vote in a key committee of the Assembly, not a single member voted to pass the bill out of committee. The powerful tobacco industry lobbyists had seemingly won.

Jane recalled, "That was the turning point. Our supporters were so outraged that it was decided in the hallway outside the hearing room to put a tobacco tax initiative on the 1988 statewide ballot." It was a herculean volunteer effort to get the signatures to qualify the initiative for the ballot and, once Proposition 99 qualified, the $20 to $30 million budgeted by big tobacco against the measure appeared to overwhelm the $1.7 million proponents had to spend. With public support for Proposition 99 dwindling shortly before election day, City Councilmember Lynn Robie, in her role as Smoking Cessation Director for the Lung Association, came up with a memorable appeal to voters. She suggested that individuals dying from illnesses caused by smoking might be willing to speak up against the industry and for smoking cessation funding. Victims of big tobacco agreed and, though there was little money to buy ads, radio and TV stations covered the story of dying victims' pleas because their message was so powerful. Proposition 99 passed with 56% of the vote.

The tobacco industry knew it had a formidable foe. In 1990, after the Lung Association and its allies convinced the Sacramento City Council and Board of Supervisors to pass ordinances "establishing a smoke-free rule for all indoor public and private workplaces and buildings open to the public, including banks, stores, terminals, buses, taxis, theaters, hospitals, recreational, and licensed daycare facilities," the tobacco industry waged war. When Sacramento County decided to place the recently passed smoke-free ordinance on the ballot for voter approval in 1992, the tobacco industry waged an expensive and deceptive campaign to defeat Measure G. Yet the voters approved the County's smoker restrictions by a comfortable margin.

The University of California Press E-Books Collection for 1982 to 2004, under the subject, *The Battle Over Local Tobacco Control Ordinances,* acknowledged the skill of Sacramento's trailblazing women and the Lung Association when it stated, "The most significant factor in Sacramento's success was the strong connection between the American Lung Association of Sacramento-Emigrant Trails and community leaders. The Sacramento ALA had recruited influential civic leaders from various backgrounds to serve on its 35 member board of directors." In 1990, when the City and County smoke-free ordinances were passed, Anne Rudin was mayor and four other women served on the city council: Heather Fargo, Lyla Ferris, Kim Mueller, and Lynn Robie. Supervisor Illa Collin was also a vocal supporter of County passage of its smoke free ordinance.

Hagedorn was proving to be a powerhouse in the way she identified problems, studied possible solutions, and went into action to convince the public to support proposed remedies. But her greatest skill was in bringing people together, first in her living room, next as an advisor to many of the elected women discussed in this book, then in the conference room of the American Lung Association of Sacramento-Emigrant Trails.

A master at putting people together who might not normally play on the same team, Jane and other key leaders also built coalitions to advance light rail development, streamline the County land use planning process, upgrade flood protection, promote cleaner fuels such as methane and compressed natural gas, and plant and maintain Sacramento's beloved canopy of trees.

The Sacramento Railway Depot

When the Sacramento Railway Depot opened, *Railway Age* called it "one of the most modern structures on the Pacific coast and one of the finest structures in Sacramento." The Depot featured a high, vaulted ceiling, massive chandeliers, travertine tile and marble floors, and a huge John A. MacQuarrie mural depicting the groundbreaking for the western terminus of the transcontinental railroad in Sacramento. It was a depot worthy of a city so strongly identified with railroad history.

The year was 1926.

By the twenty-first century, the depot was still in use, but the wear and tear of almost 75 years had left its mark. Journalist Tony Bizjak recalled in *The Sacramento Bee:*

> The depot is the seventh busiest train station in the national Amtrak system, and the second busiest west of Chicago. Despite that, many areas had fallen into disrepair. For years, rows of back offices sat empty, paneling slumping from the walls. Broken windows allowed pigeons to lay claim to upper floors. The building had no air conditioning or fire sprinklers. The roof leaked. Plaster walls were crumbling.

Moreover, Union Pacific (which bought Southern Pacific in 1996) and Amtrak had needs the old station and track configuration could not accommodate. All of this brought Sacramento to a point most cities face sooner or later. Is it time to bid goodbye to the decaying remnant of a prior era in favor of a modern, functional, more useful—if less charming—structure? Or should we try to save it?

Making such a decision is tailor-made for conflict. As Bizjak described it at the time: "The fight pits a transit group, including Union Pacific and Amtrak, against a grass-roots coalition headed by preservationists." At the forefront of those preservationists was one of Sacramento's active political women, Kay Knepprath, chair of a group called Save Our Rail Depot (SORD), organized in 2000.

A smart, charming mother of four and by then a grandmother, Knepprath had been a trusted advisor to many of Sacramento's trailblazing elected women and was a longtime leader of historic preservation. "Our heritage was being destroyed," she said, describing Union Pacific's treatment of the building as "demolition by neglect."

During those years of neglect, the 244-acre railyard site had become a visual blight and toxic wasteland caused by 150 years of railroad ownership. Separated from Old Sacramento by the I-5 freeway, the area was the site of a 26-year clean-up effort by Union Pacific under the direction of the State of California and the federal Environmental Protection Agency, finally completed in early 2020.

Various promising projects had been proposed for the railyard over the years, negotiated over, and ultimately falling through, including a baseball stadium (eventually built in West Sacramento), a new basketball arena (voted down in an election), and development proposals eventually abandoned because of the protracted clean-up process.

How did the fight to save the depot proceed under Kay Knepprath's leadership? "Meetings in the dining room of my house," Knepprath says now. "You don't do it by yourself. You do it by convincing a lot of other people it should be done. We organized SORD with 24 organizations concerned with transportation, good government, neighborhoods, and preservation."

One supporter observed, "The Save Our Rail Depot coalition has enlisted the support of many key political leaders (past and present), neighborhood associations, hundreds of concerned rail users and preservationists and, indeed, anyone provided the opportunity to grasp the potential of the railyard."

Knepprath chose her language strategically. The depot was a "classy 1920s gem." Those against preserving the historic depot were "transit bureaucrats." Union Pacific and Amtrak modeled their plan for a proposed new depot to match others they had built; SORD called them "Amshaks." She described the negotiators from Union Pacific as people "whose minds and hearts are in ice in Omaha."

In 2006, the city purchased the depot from Union Pacific (UP), a commitment that increased the demand for a decision on its fate. Alternative solutions abounded:

- Using the depot for Greyhound bus service and building a new train terminal
- Using it for city buses and light rail
- Building a new depot and renting out the old one for shops
- Restoring it as a venue for community activities such as an auditorium or museum
- Moving the tracks north as UP desired, then hoisting the 7000-pound depot onto rollers and moving it closer to the new tracks

SORD drew up plans to build longer passenger platforms behind the station, moving the tracks to make room for that. Knepprath argued that the plan drafted by SORD met Amtrak requirements, adjusted for UP freight train needs, and increased passenger safety by distancing freight lines from passenger lines.

By this time, another of Sacramento's women leaders became involved. In reality, representatives of the two sides would not speak to one another; yet Mayor Heather Fargo said, "The sense I have is that the sides are not as far apart as they portray themselves to be." The city sponsored a working group with representatives from each side and carefully built consensus.

When concerns over the depot began to be public in the late '90s, the building was almost 75 years old. After conflicting visions, needs, and technical difficulties were resolved, the city began renovation of the building in 2014, while making plans for an Intermodal Transit Facility and continuing the complex planning process for the largest infill site in the United States. Today, what is now called the Sacramento Valley Station welcomes over one million visitors a year. Speaking of her time as chair of the SORD effort, Kay says with a sense of pride intermixed with relief, "The depot would have been destroyed if we hadn't done it."

As to the remainder of The Railyards site, an area equal in size to Sacramento's central business district, an ambitious master plan has been adopted by the city that provides for a 20,000 seat major league soccer stadium that anchors the mixed use urban landscape, attracting tech workers and tourists and providing up to 10,000 residential units and 70,000 square feet of retail space. A new County courthouse is planned, as is a new hospital, museum, and farmers' market—celebrating Sacramento's most recent definition as "farm to fork capital" of the United States.

Turn Back to the Future

Sacramento in the '60s and '70s was grappling with the effects of rapid population growth reflected in suburban sprawl, leading to construction of more and more freeways clogged with a never-ending supply of cars, producing dangerous levels of smog. Public transit use declined as low density land use made it more and more difficult to provide efficient service. It seemed that there would be no end to this spiral of growth, freeway construction, and congestion.

At the time, the State Department of Transportation (Caltrans) saw its role as primarily to build freeways and had submitted plans to the city and county of Sacramento to build three more freeways through Carmichael and Fair Oaks, with three crossings over the American River. Several local public servants and volunteer groups joined together in opposition to freeways that would destroy whole neighborhoods, cause air pollution, intrude on the American River Parkway, cut people off from each other, and uproot many from their homes. Public hearings revealed that opposition to the freeways had galvanized the public and, despite support for the freeways by the County Department of Public Works, the Board of Supervisors voted to delete the freeways from transportation plans and consider alternatives. Likewise, the City of Sacramento, spurred on by citizen groups, re-examined the wisdom of completing construction of the I-80 Bypass in North Sacramento, intended as a relief valve for the highly congested I-80 freeway, and eventually submitted a formal request to the federal government to shift funding from freeway construction to transit.

The proposal to expand public transit was rooted in a relatively new concept in the United States: light rail transit (LRT), a much less costly alternative to subway construction. In Sacramento, a small cadre of streetcar enthusiasts set out to educate the community about LRT after returning from a fact-finding trip to major Northern European cities, where new urban trolley systems were a vital link in modern vibrant cities.

Led by Ruth and Wayne Hultgren (the "Father of Light Rail Transit"), the Modern Transit Society began a grassroots campaign to advance new thinking about freeways and transit in 1975. They made speeches about the merits of "light rail transit" (LRT) with impressive slide shows before a myriad of groups and held informational sessions with appointed and elected officials, as well as community activists and planners. They emphasized that while light rail had some similarities to the once successful Sacramento trolley system—dismantled in 1947 by a consortium of oil, tire, and automotive interests (in favor of buses)—the modern European systems were different. They were not clanging one-car anachronisms, but quiet trains, semi-segregated from traffic, with huge doors and efficient fare systems, serving city centers teeming with pedestrians.

At the time, only a few North American cities had considered substituting LRT for freeways: Edmonton and Calgary in Alberta, Canada (opened in 1978 and 1981 respectively); San Diego,

California (opened in 1981); and Portland, Oregon (opened in 1986). But citizens in more and more cities were becoming disillusioned by the neighborhood destruction, noise, and pollution caused by automobiles and freeway construction and were willing to consider transit alternatives.

At the urging of the Modern Transit Society, the American Lung Association, the Sierra Club, the Environmental Council of Sacramento, the League of Women Voters, and various volunteer civic groups, the City Council and Board of Supervisors made a historic decision in 1976 to turn their backs on more freeway construction, when they requested that federal funds for freeway construction be allocated instead for a light rail line.

Federal law required that an alternatives analysis and Environmental Impact Report (EIR) be completed before funding could be shifted to transit. In mid–1981, an alternatives analysis and EIR were completed. They envisioned an 18.3 mile "starter line" using existing rights of way and proven off-the-shelf technology to reduce costs; and building low cost, functional stations. The route would start in the northeast area at Watt Avenue, use the abandoned I-80 Bypass paralleling I-80, run along downtown streets (where two pedestrian malls were planned), and run next to Folsom Boulevard, terminating at Butterfield Avenue. The old and often maligned "tank trap" structures of K Street Mall would be torn down to allow for a LRT/pedestrian mall.

Although 47 different community groups endorsed selection of LRT in 1981, there was plenty of opposition to the project, including Regional Transit's (RT) Board and top management, the City Traffic Engineer, the County Department of Public Works, the Sacramento Area Council of Governments, and some residential and business groups who feared the disruption that construction would bring. In 1980–81, a new RT Board of Directors was put in place, senior management was fired, and a new general manager with experience in the design and construction of the Bay Area Rapid Transit (BART) system was hired to reorganize the agency and patch up negative public opinion of RT.

Doubts remained as to RT's ability to design and construct the project on time and within budget, so a joint powers authority comprising RT, the City, the County, and Caltrans was set up in 1981 to oversee design, construction, procurement, and operator training. The new agency was named the Sacramento Transit Development Agency (STDA). The problem was, it wasn't clear where the proverbial buck stopped. Who was responsible when the inevitable budget shortfall was identified? Political controversy and recrimination ensued after the 1983 LRT budget of $131 million was found to be seriously underestimated.

An outside analyst was recruited to examine budget estimates, pinpoint problems with STDA's line of command, and identify corrective measures, resulting in a recommendation to transfer project responsibility to RT in 1985. But two revised budgets, first at $156 million in 1985, then a final estimate of $176 million, were met with skepticism. To make up the $45 million budget deficit, the City of Sacramento and the Sacramento Housing and Redevelopment Agency issued certificates of participation. Naysayers in the business, political, and news communities asked, "Why are we doing this?" "Can't we stop the project now and cut our losses?" (Cameron Beach, *A Success Story That Was Not Supposed to Happen*). But it was too late to halt the project. Twenty-six LRT vehicles had been ordered; utility relocation was well underway; rail, ties, special trackwork, and overhead electrical cable had begun arriving; and three miles of light rail track was in place. Construction of the "largest public works project ever undertaken in the area" (Beach) went full steam ahead.

Caltrans design staff, construction managers, community relations staff, and other critical support staff worked overtime to get the project built by the planned opening date of March 12, 1987. The newly hired LRT project manager was a genius at team building, with a laser-like focus on getting the job done, while urging open and respectful information sharing. Some likened the team effort to a NASA space program; it even had a countdown calendar marking the days and tasks to be completed by the planned system-opening in 1987.

A technical advisory team, including staunch opponents like the City Traffic Engineer, met regularly to anticipate and mitigate the effects of construction on critical municipal services. Likewise, a downtown citizens' advisory committee, including business, government, retail, and residential interests, met regularly.

Public celebrations were held to mark major milestones in the project, such as a groundbreaking ceremony and tree relocation event for the new K Street Transit Mall (March 1984), with an auction of four mature trees from the old mall to benefit the Sacramento Tree Foundation and highlight the purchase of 1730 trees to landscape the train route and stations (including 90 for K Street Mall). In April 1985, a ceremony was held to drive the first spike. June 10, 1986, was the occasion for community leaders to ride the first RT Metro train in Sacramento. Most guests had never ridden on a light rail train and the newness of it was exciting.

By late 1986, K Street businesses had been disrupted for nearly two years by unsightly plywood fences erected to protect the public from demolition of the old mall and by the nearly constant sound of heavy construction equipment destroying the old and building the new. A November 25, 1986, *Sacramento Bee* advertising headline for its special publication, Office Hours, read, "The Fences Come Down." Inside the publication were news stories about the renovation of the Crest Theater, interviews with the public about their attitudes toward the new mall, and announcements of public events planned to mark the near-completion of the new mall. A four-day "K Street Celebration" featured speeches, a ribbon-cutting, food fair, music, entertainment, the display of a light rail car, and free bus rides.

On opening day for the largest public works project Sacramento had ever undertaken, the first electric train to operate in the state capital in over 40 years proceeded toward downtown. Large crowds gathered at every station to applaud, and the following weekend over 200,000 people took advantage of the opportunity to experience LRT for the first time. Despite the skeptics and budget controversies, the cost of Sacramento's light rail system came in at $10 million per mile, the lowest per mile cost of any LRT system in the United States. As then-Mayor Anne Rudin recalled, "public support for light rail was the most widespread and unified that I had ever seen."

Of critical importance to public understanding of the project was the establishment and hard work of a public/private partnership, Friends of Light Rail (FOLR), founded in 1985. It included a broad range of community and business leaders and was set up to help educate the public about light rail and raise money for artwork and landscaping. A major goal of the LRT project was to recognize the unique quality of each neighborhood served by light rail through the planting of trees at LRT stations and installation of public art at each station. The Sacramento Metropolitan Arts Commission was enlisted to screen proposals, supervise completion of the artworks, and coordinate installation. After 32 years, the artwork lives on.

After the system opened in 1987, FOLR members and the organizations they represented were in the forefront of the drive to raise more local matching dollars to help expand the system. Measure A asked voters to support a 1/2 cent sales tax on the November 1988 ballot. If passed by the local electorate, every one dollar raised by the sales tax would be matched by three dollars of federal funding for light rail construction or procurement. Measure A passed, and FOLR was instrumental in expansion of the system that now includes service to the City of Folsom, Sacramento City College, and Cosumnes River College, for a total of 42.9 miles and 54 stations.

As Cameron Beach, in charge of light rail maintenance at the time, put it, "Citizens who made comments in the early 1980s like, 'Why are we doing this?' changed their tune. The new battle cry became, 'Who gets the next extension?'"

Throughout the 11 years from inception to service opening, female community leaders such as Anne Rudin, Illa Collin, Lynn Robie, and Lyla Ferris remained stalwart supporters of light rail. FOLR, under the wings of Ruth and Wayne Hultgren, Jean Runyon, Jane Hagedorn, Ann Kohl, Linda Budge, and many others was a driving force for system expansion and enhancement. In 2018, FOLR celebrated 31 years of light rail and transit service in a community now defined, in part, by its turn back to the future.

Advancing the Arts

There is NO great city without arts enrichment.

— Former County Supervisor Muriel Johnson

The welcoming sign at the intersection of the East Sacramento and River Park communities of Sacramento declares, "Great Art Makes A Great Community." Not far from the sign, on Fair Oaks Blvd. in the Pavilions shopping center, a life-size stoneware sculpture of a mother with her two children, by ceramicist Ruth Rippon, celebrates women's traditional role in our communities. Across the American River north of downtown at Niños Park in South Natomas, an art tile project for and by children hugs the trunk of a lovely shade tree.

The web that ties art and community together is woven at many levels: the artists themselves; government and non-profit groups that work to advance the arts; elected and appointed officials; individual patrons of the arts; ticket holders to live performances; operators of and visitors to museums and galleries; grass roots and neighborhood organizations, schools, and universities; journalists and art critics; civic-minded business people; and the natural human urge to beautify and make our world a better place to live.

Our focus in *We Can Do This!* is on a number of pioneering women who came together during a singular period in Sacramento, when the region was remaking itself from its "cow town" image to that of a vibrant arts community, inclusive of both men and women.

One such woman is Sacramento-born ceramicist Ruth Rippon, who found her calling while studying at the California College of Arts and Crafts in Oakland and became the first female member of the art department faculty at Sacramento State College (later CSUS) in 1956, where she founded the ceramics program. Rippon is known and recognized as an inspirational teacher, mentor to young artists, and prolific creator of ceramic art. The female figures conjured up by Rippon for her bowls, plates, vases, and sculptures reflect both timelessness in their references to Greek and Roman mythologies and flash points of unrest in the turbulence of American culture and politics.

The art world was mostly a man's world in the '60s and '70s, so Ruth Rippon's recognition as the first artist, male or female, honored with a retrospective show and catalogue at the E. B. Crocker Art Gallery (later Crocker Art Museum) in 1971 was a singular achievement. A later retrospective at the Crocker in 2017, *Exuberant Earth—Ceramics by Ruth Rippon* (catalogue written by Kristina Perea Gilmore and Jo Lauria), attests to her continuing artistic contribution to Sacramento, as well as to California and the nation as a whole. "Because of her own work, and her influence as a teacher, she is one of the artists most responsible for the Sacramento Valley's reputation as a creative center for the ceramic arts." (Driesbach, Willoughby, and Moore. *Material Witness: Masters from California Craft*, 1999, p.34).

Rippon was also a community and arts activist as an early member of the Creative Arts League Sacramento (CALS), founded in 1952 by 10 women to showcase local contemporary artists. In 1952, there were no private galleries in Sacramento, making it difficult for the work of local artists to be seen and appreciated. CALS addressed this deficit by locating exhibition spaces and staging about 30 one-person shows per year.

In the late '50s, CALS approached the Crocker with a proposal that CALS sponsor, finance, and organize a statewide competitive show in 1959 for fine craft artists. The term "fine craft artist" was a relatively new one, in recognition that the historically rigid separation of fine arts from crafts was finally breaking down. With the introduction of new materials and technologies, the line between art and craft was blurred, and wonderfully innovative new artists such as Ruth Rippon emerged both in Sacramento and at the University of California at Davis.

The aesthetic and popular success of the 1959 exhibition (later named *California Crafts 1*) led to biennial craft shows at the Crocker and other CALS-sponsored shows elsewhere in the region for nearly 60 years. In recognition of her important role in advancing the arts, CALS designated Ruth Rippon as a "California Living Treasure" in 2002 and she was honored by Mayor Heather Fargo and the Sacramento City Council.

The resolve and success of civic-minded women who loved the arts in the '50s and '60s led to more formal government structures and programs to advance the arts in the '70s. One such City and County entity is the Sacramento Metropolitan Arts Commission (SMAC), founded in 1977 with funding from the state and federal government. The woman most instrumental in organizing and launching the programs of SMAC is Susan Willoughby, appointed in 1977 by Mayor Phil Isenberg as Special Assistant to the Mayor, an unpaid position she held for six years. At the time, the city budget did not fund many paid staff positions in support of elected officials. The mayor had a secretary and the rest of the city council shared just one secretary. Thus, innovative programs were sometimes set in motion by generous individuals dedicated to a program's mission. As a long-serving member of CALS, art collector, and college art instructor, Susan came to symbolize what one smart and dedicated advocate for the arts can do.

At the outset, Willoughby formed an advisory committee to consider how the Arts Commission should be appointed and organized. An initial proposal to ask the City and County to appoint four representatives each, plus one to represent the cities of Folsom, Isleton, and Galt, was amended by Sandra Smoley, the first woman to be elected to the Board of Supervisors. She felt each of the five elected supervisors should be able to appoint a member to the Commission. Thus, from its start, the Arts Commission came to be viewed as important and potentially controversial. Smoley appointed arts advocate and future supervisor Muriel Johnson to the Arts Commission in 1977.

One program administered by SMAC was part of the federally funded Comprehensive Employment and Training Act (CETA). The purpose of the Act was to train unemployed people to move into the larger work force. Creative thinkers convinced the City Council, the administrators of the local fund, that being a working artist was a real job. So six positions were set aside for full-time working artists, something like the Work Progress Administration (WPA) of the '30s. And when the program was over, most artists positively transitioned to paying jobs.

A key component of the Metropolitan Arts Commission is the Art in Public Places Program (APP), by which "2% of eligible City and County capital improvement projects is set aside for the commission, purchase, and installation of artworks throughout the City" (California Arts Council website). One of the first artists to be awarded a commission through the APP program was Fred Uhl Ball, for an enamel mural to be installed on the west-facing wall of the four-story downtown parking garage near Macy's. Titled *The Way Home*, it was the largest hand-fired mural in the world when it was installed in 1980. Ball's mural was intended to "remind viewers of the ongoing joy of life" (SMAC website), and it continues to do so after its 2012 restoration, evoking the play of light over Sacramento's rivers and fields. Ball's love of the region and of art was inspired by his mother, Kathryn Uhl, a Sacramento native and one of only a few prominent Northern California female printmakers. Citing the need to maintain and, if needed, restore other works of public art in the region, Susan Willoughby cautioned that funding for such maintenance needed to be strengthened.

Similarly, former City Council member, Kim Mueller (District 6, 1988–92), lamented the awkward interface in the art selection and installation process by city public works and planning staff that has occasionally resulted in a wonderful piece of public art not working properly or being nearly invisible to the public. For example, the City ultimately turned off the water source for the Roger Berry water fountain at the corner of the 10th and I Street parking garage because it often broke. Mueller cited another unsuccessful piece—"the gorgeous glass mobile/chandelier" in the Tsakopoulos Gallery at the downtown main library which remains unlit because of new energy efficiency standards—and urged managers of SMAC and the Art in Public Places Program to "think through all of these issues in advance with the artist as a full team player at the table."

Both Mueller and Heather Fargo raised concerns about perceived slights to local artists when major expensive commissions went to out-of-town artists, rather than local artists. With that in mind, when construction of a new City Hall was in the planning stages, Mayor Fargo insisted that the art in City Hall be only Sacramento-focused art by Sacramento artists. SMAC resisted, "but I insisted that art in the city's house should not include ocean scenes, or tall mountains, or any other images not about our city, and that a civic building project should support our own artists, and not one from NYC. I prevailed."

SMAC's mission is to "support education, equity and the economy" (SMAC website). Equity was a major focus for Deborah Ortiz, who became the first elected Latina city councilmember in 1993.

A native of Sacramento, and granddaughter of Mexican immigrants who settled in the area in the 1930s, Ortiz was raised by a mother who urged her to strive for excellence and fight for justice. In her oversight role on the City Council, Ortiz wanted to make sure a fair share of money generated for the arts would go to underserved and underrepresented groups. Ortiz was a strong supporter of La Posada, the Latino Center of Arts & Culture, founded in 1972 "to promote and preserve the art and culture of the Chicano, Latino and Native American community" (La Posada website).

Likewise, Heather Fargo (who served with Ortiz) recognized the economic development power of the arts and focused on "equity, or the lack thereof, in many of Sacramento's neighborhoods and diverse populations." Looking back at her tenure on the Council, Heather expressed pride in her early support for, promotion of, and participation in Festival de la Familia and the Pacific Rim Street Fest, large events which celebrated cultural and artistic diversity.

Noting that the downtown commercial core often receives the lion's share of public funding for art, Fargo fought successfully to bring some of those funds to her neighborhood of South Natomas. Likewise, Lyla Ferris fought for her North Sacramento community and started the first annual Hagginwood Summer Festival at Hagginwood Park in Del Paso Heights. Ferris recalled that she especially enjoyed the Gospel Music Day, featuring church and community choirs from the surrounding neighborhoods.

The goal of bringing music to the neighborhoods where people live and work was advanced spectacularly by Councilmembers Lauren Hammond (elected to serve District 5, 1997-2010) and Bonnie Pannell (elected to serve District 8, 1999-2015), who brought jazz concerts to the Oak Park and Meadowview communities, respectively. Hammond, the first Black woman ever elected to the Sacramento City Council, put neighborhood equity at the top of her priority list. Hammond's support of the Oak Park Concert Series (started by former Councilmember Callie Carney, appointed to represent District 5 from 1976–78) was a win for local restaurants, performers, and audiences alike. Hammond was named one of Sacramento's 30 "Most Powerful Women" by *Sacramento Magazine* in 2007.

Bonnie Pannell first ran for City Council in 1998, following the death of her husband, Sam, who served on the Council from 1993 to 1998. Like her husband, Bonnie was determined that the Black community get a fair shake. During her 16 years on the Council, she prioritized economic development, safer neighborhoods, and better education in her South Sacramento district. According to the *Sacramento Observer*, "For many years, Bonnie Pannell organized the Meadowview Jazz and Cultural Festival and made it one of Sacramento's most anticipated entertainment events" (Genoa Barrow, *Former Sacramento City Councilmember Bonnie Pannell Passes, Sacramento Observer*, June 27, 2017). Staging the event at Cosumnes River College (CRC) was a double victory, since Bonnie is also remembered for her advocacy and success in bringing light rail transit service to CRC beginning in August 2015.

Former Mayor Heather Fargo and retiring Councilmember Bonnie Pannell at Pannell's good-bye party at Sacramento City Hall, 2014

Photo by Larry Dalton

In a bid to "give people a reason to come or stay downtown in a way that was fun and comfortable," Heather Fargo started the Friday Night Concert Series at Plaza Park (now Cesar Chavez Park) in 1991 in cooperation with the new Downtown District. At the time, Plaza Park was a gathering place for the homeless population, but after, as Fargo put it, "meeting with the homeless over donuts to get them to move to one corner and behave themselves," the concerts were successfully staged before enthusiastic audiences.

Fargo, a strong supporter of the rights of marginalized communities, also enthusiastically supported the Sacramento Gay Men's Chorus, an integral part of Sacramento's LGBTQ+ community since 1984, "fostering pride and enhancing lives one song at a time."

Bringing the arts to school children was a high priority for local elected women. Heather Fargo cited her support of funding for the Crocker Art Museum's mobile Art Ark, which visits schools in neighborhoods throughout the city. Both Fargo and Mueller appeared with the Sacramento Symphony to narrate *Peter and the Wolf* before wide-eyed children and their parents in neighborhood parks. Another enduring tradition of the Sacramento Symphony (now the Sacramento Philharmonic and Opera) and the Sacramento Ballet is *The Nutcracker*, which gives aspiring young singers and dancers a chance to soar as they work with their adult professional peers. As part of their roles as city councilmembers, both Mueller and Lyla Ferris were costumed participants in the opening scene of *The Nutcracker*.

Long before winning election to the Sacramento County Board of Supervisors in 2004, Muriel Johnson brought her passion for music to the children of Sacramento by facilitating the Tiny Tots Concerts in the late 1960s. As part of several programs to bring classical music to children of all ages, the Sacramento Symphony formed a 40-member "Little Symphony," performing short concerts for children age three to six years old. Seated on the floor, while surrounded by the performers, the children were invited to talk to the musicians and touch their instruments after the concerts. With her background as a music major in college, high school vocal music teacher, and member of the Sacramento Symphony League, Muriel Johnson was the ideally suited volunteer to lead the program.

Muriel Johnson has been an avid supporter of the arts in Sacramento since moving here in 1962, including as a co-founder of the Sacramento Metropolitan Arts Commission in 1977. Throughout her life—as a music teacher, many years as a community volunteer, founding member of the Sacramento Region Community Foundation (1983), 12 years of service on the Sacramento County Board of Supervisors (1992–2004), and seven years as Director of the California Arts

L to R: Supervisors Muriel Johnson, Sandra Smoley and Susan Peters at the end of a nearly 50-year dynasty of women leading Sacramento's District 3, October 2020.

Council (2005–2011)—Johnson has put the arts front and center. She is especially proud of her role in raising more than $10 million for local charities, community service projects, and the arts, including the first Crocker Art Museum expansion. Recognized and honored by Congressman Robert Matsui in 2004 for her commitment to improving the community, Johnson was also awarded a Lifetime Achievement Award in 2011 from the California Arts Council for her work to advance the arts at the state and local level.

The two women who originally broke the all-male glass ceiling by successfully running for local office in 1971 and 1972, Anne Rudin and Sandra Smoley, are regarded as unwavering and highly effective advocates for the Sacramento Symphony, especially when it faced labor and funding crises. Explaining that "Anne definitely was the leader in efforts to maintain the Symphony," Kim Mueller recalled "a time when a number of us, with Anne as the lead voice, strove to ensure the arts were appreciated and well enough funded, but it was often an uphill battle."

Women artists in particular faced an uphill battle in the '60s, '70s, and '80s, when men dominated the art world and were the gatekeepers at museums and galleries. Women artists, especially those with spouses and children, found it difficult to carve out the time and space to create their art, get it seen, receive public recognition in the form of reviews, and be hired as instructors at the college level. Ruth Rippon's success in securing a teaching position at Sacramento State was a rarity in an era when men controlled hiring and tended to hire men just like themselves. For example, one male U.C. Davis art faculty member, interviewing a female applicant for a sculpture teaching job, stated that despite her advanced degrees and obvious qualifications, she wouldn't be able hold her own in the physically demanding sculpture department. She promptly demonstrated her strength by picking up a hefty, overstuffed armchair. She got the job.

Recognizing the isolation and obstacles that women artists face, 15 local female artists got together in 1977 to provide a supportive environment for women. Matrix Workshop of Women Artists offered classes, constructive critiques, workshops, and lectures when it first opened on Broadway in Oak Park. A lack of self-confidence often plagued women artists, so Matrix's practical advice that members increase their visibility by taking slides of their work and submitting them to competitive shows was invaluable. Matrix's role in empowering women was significant; by 1990, Matrix was mentoring 100 members.

Matrix created opportunities for women to display their art by opening a gallery at its new home at Sierra 2 Center for the Arts on 24th Street in the early '80s, after the abandoned school was saved from demolition and renovated. The renovation work for Matrix was spearheaded by the women and, in an ironic twist, the male partners of Matrix women were given T-shirts emblazoned with the words, Matrix Auxiliary.

Advancements in the arts by and for women have often been made in spite of male prejudice and disdain. Pam Johnson, a Sacramento native and co-founder of Matrix, summoned a familiar quote to counsel women that "courage isn't the absence of fear, but having fear and moving forward anyway." But sometimes stepping forward seems to come in baby steps. A 1989 poster produced by Guerrilla Girls,

Conscience of the Art World, asked, "Do women have to be naked to get into the Met Museum?" The poster went on to proclaim that "Less than 5% of the artists in the Modern Art sections are women, but 85% of the nudes are female." Guerrilla Girls was founded to fight discrimination against women artists and artists of color in the art world. It was inspired to fight the white, male-dominated art world when it was discovered that a major 1985 exhibition at the Metropolitan Museum of Art in New York City, *An International Survey of Painting and Sculpture*, featured 148 men, only 13 women, and no artists of color. Salt was added to the wound when the curator of the show said that "any artist who wasn't in the show should rethink *his* career."

Art and urban revitalization often go hand in hand. City Councilmember Kim Mueller played a key role in the development of the fledgling arts district of Del Paso Blvd. in North Sacramento. Mueller helped lay the groundwork for the "Phantom Galleries" project, which was launched shortly after she left office in the early '90s. A precursor to modern pop-up restaurants and events, Phantom art shows were held in empty spaces and conveyed a certain mystery and excitement, "attracting hundreds if not thousands of people, young and old" (Mueller).

Mueller also encouraged the relocation of the highly regarded contemporary art gallery, the Michael Himovitz Gallery, from its downtown location to a former furniture store on Del Paso Blvd. With financial assistance from the Sacramento Housing and Redevelopment Agency (SHRA), the building, which had more space than was needed by the gallery, was purchased. Mueller explained that "the vision was that with subtenants, the gallery could achieve self-sufficiency and an equity stake. With delays in subtenant occupancy and Michael Himovitz's untimely death, that vision faded."

After she left the Council in the fall of 1992, Mueller continued to champion artists and the arts. Recognizing the difficulty artists have in finding affordable live and workspaces, Mueller worked to facilitate construction of an artist-owned live-work community, named SurrealEstates, in North Sacramento. SurrealEstates was finally built in the early 2000s with the support of District 2 councilmembers Rob Kerth (1992-2000) and Sandy Sheedy (2000-2012) with financial assistance from SHRA. In a personal commitment to advancing the arts, Mueller and her husband converted a building they owned on Del Paso Blvd. into 14 studios that were offered to artists at below market rates. She explained, "In all my efforts in North Sacramento, my goal was to ensure artists had a seat at the table and could share in any economic growth that followed their adopting and improving an area that previously had declined."

Estelle Saltzman and Jean Runyon, friends and partners for 35 years in the powerful Runyon Saltzman public relations firm, found a novel way to both serve a client's interests and promote the visual arts. In the mid-'70s, their firm was hired by Regional Transit (RT) to promote bus service and improve RT's image. Saltzman explained:

> We came up with the idea of conducting a mobile Bus Bench Art Show to draw positive attention to RT and to increase ridership. With help from RT, we provided willing artists with seven-foot long blank bus bench backs used normally for advertising messages. On the day the newly designed bus bench backs were put in place at various downtown sites, we invited print, radio, and television news people, along with several art aficionados and city officials, to join us at/on our traveling 'art opening' via an RT bus. For our first show, we left it up to the artists to decorate their individual benches any way they wanted, but in second and third shows, we established themes, such as preserving the environment.

After each opening, the art benches stayed up for two months and then the artists were able to sell their artworks. Saltzman is the proud owner of several delightful bench backs.

Jean Runyon's devotion to the Sacramento theater scene was unparalleled. Runyon's first break as a young aspiring public relations professional occurred in the early 1950s, when Runyon was recruited by Eleanor McClatchy to sell Music Circus group theater packages. From that point on, until a year before her death in 2009, she bought season tickets to the Music Circus and other productions of the Sacramento Theater Company (STC). When Runyon and Saltzman became partners in the early 1970s, Estelle also bought season tickets, and when they were unable to attend a performance, each gave their tickets to their young employees, who might not have ever attended live musical theater of any kind.

STC was founded by Eleanor McClatchy as the Sacramento Civic Repertory Theatre in 1942 as a touring company to entertain locally stationed troops during World War II. In 1949, it emerged as the Eaglet Theatre and, in 1951, began staging Broadway at Music Circus in a large, round tent erected just for these summer shows. The Music Circus was a hybrid that combined the informality of a circus, mostly unobstructed views for the audience, and the summer-camp charm of a Chautauqua theatre. The theater group incorporated as the Sacramento Light Opera Association in 1953. In the1980s, STC became a professional theater company and, in 2003, with support from City loans promoted by Mayor Heather Fargo, it moved into the Wells Fargo Pavilion, a modern theater complex at 15th and H Street that includes an in-the-round building for Music Circus productions on the site of the old tent. Jean Runyon and Estelle Saltzman played a major role in the continuous advancement of the Sacramento Theater Company.

In a fitting tribute to Jean's love of Sacramento and the theater, the community loved her back. Recognizing the need to renovate the Little Theater in the Memorial Auditorium, a group of Jean's friends approached the City with the idea to raise restoration funds through private donations. The City agreed and, in a birthday surprise for

Runyon's 70th birthday, a crowd of 300 friends unveiled plans to raise $300,000 for the project and rename the theater, The Jean Runyon Little Theater. Naturally, Jean pitched in and raised a significant amount of money herself! Estelle Saltzman recalled that, "At the end of the effort, a small amount of unallocated money was deposited in Jean's name in an account at the Sacramento Region Community Foundation."

The important role of women in advancing the arts is indisputable. Without their vision, generosity, and perseverance, the diversity of Sacramento's culture and art would not be the wellspring of community pride it is today.

Legacy

I want to be remembered as a woman...who dared to be a catalyst of change.
—Shirley Chisholm, First African American woman to
seek the Democratic party nomination for president
of the United States, 1972

While the achievements of Sacramento's trailblazing women are visible throughout the city and county—in the form of parks, museums, community centers, attractive business districts, public art, transit lines, infrastructure, even stop signs and traffic lights—their legacy of working with others to find solutions to daunting problems, such as the effects of Proposition 13, are less visible, but equally important.

Asked to reflect on some of their proudest achievements, many women interviewed for this book cited their less-tangible achievements, having more to do with the process of problem solving and governance. For example, Councilmember Lynn Robie was proud of how she worked with her Greenhaven/Pocket neighbors to find a way to fund neighborhood schools after passage of Prop. 13 capped local property taxes. Taking advantage of a statewide act (Mello-Roos, passed in 1982) that allowed communities to tax themselves outside of the limits of Prop. 13, Robie and a small group of dedicated volunteers led passage of Measure U with a 2/3 vote approving the issuance of bonds to finance public schools. That meant that citizens were willing to raise their taxes to build schools for their children and their neighbors' children.

Each and every woman cited her commitment to improving poorer neighborhoods in their districts. Their efforts helped eliminate blight and bring new businesses to long-neglected areas. Councilmember Lauren Hammond recalled, "We brought the first grocery store in Oak Park in thirty years. And we closed and razed two liquor stores that were the most troubled sites in their neighborhood." Her immediate District 5 predecessor, Deborah Ortiz, recalled being sued by an Oak Park liquor store owner for her attempts to curtail drug dealing in the store's parking lot. Ortiz made a regular habit of inspecting the streets and alleyways of Oak Park for accumulated trash and landlord neglect, informing city Code Enforcement of her findings, and in some cases closing alleys that were chronic trouble spots. Ortiz also expressed pride in leading the 15-year clean-up of toxic waste in the Curtis Park railroad yards, paving the way for significant in-fill development, including new housing and retail services.

High value was placed on constituent relations, including regular outreach to people on their own turf. Although former Supervisor Sandy Smoley was clearly proud of her many years raising money for the Sacramento Symphony (prior to, during, and after serving on the Board), she clearly relished meeting with her constituents in Rio Linda, Elverta, and North Highlands, folks who reminded her of her neighbors in the small Iowa town where she was raised. Driving through the neighborhoods of her district, Smoley also enjoyed seeing the visible results of her work to make the community more livable. Councilmembers Lyla Ferris and Sandy Sheedy both pointed to their efforts to deliver basic community services such as sewer service and repair of crumbling infrastructure.

Councilmembers Lauren Hammond and Sandy Sheedy recalled the satisfaction of serving on the Council's Law and Legislation Committee, which allowed good ideas to be implemented within the framework of the law. Councilmember Kim Mueller expressed pride in her service on the City's Campaign Finance Committee, leading to more transparency and public reporting of campaign contributions.

Paying Forward

Sacramento's trailblazing women pointed to the younger women they helped "bring up" in local government. Sandy Smoley said that a source of great satisfaction was her success in making sure at least one woman was appointed to each and every County board and commission during her 20-year tenure on the Board. Moreover, Smoley's bravery in going public about her breast cancer diagnosis and decision to undergo a double mastectomy continues to elicit expressions of gratitude from women who attribute Smoley's advocacy of regular mammograms to saving their own lives.

CSUS Professor Emeritus Barbara O'Connor urged younger women to "get a mentor," noting how important mentors were in her professional development. City Councilmember Deborah Ortiz also cited the importance of elected women acting as mentors to younger women, observing that women of color have another level of responsibility to support younger women of color in their aspirations to serve the community.

Asked for advice to younger aspirational women, Councilmember Lynn Robie emphasized the importance of attending City Council and Board of Supervisors meetings to gain an understanding of the governing process and issues before the council; applying to serve on local boards and commissions; and using this experience to determine if they really want to serve the long hours required of elected officials. Mayor Heather Fargo emphasized the importance of working in and for their neighborhood association or other public interest group, and applying to local boards and commissions, especially the planning commission. Fargo also stressed the value of really learning through attentive listening and development of skills in reading, writing, public speaking, and debate. For women weighing the pros and cons of running for elective office, emphasis was placed on the need to learn fundraising skills. Asking for help, especially campaign contributions, is a major hurdle for many women, one that has to be overcome. Councilmember Deborah Ortiz and Supervisor Sandra Smoley were unequivocal about the importance of learning how to raise money for good causes, including their own election.

Mayor Anne Rudin made a special point of reaching out to young girls and encouraging them to pursue their dreams. The importance of parents, grandparents, and teachers in the development of self-confidence in girls has come up repeatedly in interviews with Sacramento's trail-

Photo courtesy of Sacramento League of Women Voters

Sacramento League of Women Voters (LWV) member Trisha Uhrhammer (left) with past-presidents Anne Rudin (1960-61) and Kay Knepprath (1971-73) and member Suzanne Phinney awarding LWV Anne Rudin Scholarship to Michele Gish in 2016

blazing political women. Almost every woman interviewed for this book pointed to a key figure in her life who insisted that she could achieve whatever she set out to do. In furtherance of such moral support, in the mid-1990s, the Sacramento League of Women Voters established a college scholarship fund in honor of Anne Rudin. The purpose of the annual scholarship is to encourage and support women studying public policy and public administration. By the year 2021, the scholarship had helped 12 women pursue their dreams. Profits from the sale of this book will be donated to the Anne Rudin Scholarship Fund.

Another of Sacramento's most admired and beloved female mentors, public relations maven Jean Runyon, encouraged and helped countless local women achieve their goals. Councilmember Kim Mueller noted that "all the women elected in the early years to the Council enjoyed her critical early and full support. I know I did!" One of Runyon's memorable gestures in relating to people was to recognize and praise them by writing thank you notes. Her brief handwritten notes were cherished by the many young women and men who admired her.

In 2019, the Rotary Club of Sacramento (the club that had prohibited women from membership until 1987, when they invited Jean Runyon to be the first female member) established the Jean Runyon Community Service Award. Nominees for the honor, first awarded in 2020, are judged by the following criteria: serves the community, blazes trails, creates opportunities, gives generously, champions women in business, and has Jean Runyon leadership attributes. The Jean Runyon leadership attributes listed in the nomination form are that she or he is resilient, appreciates diversity, has a sense of humor, is an influencer, is a good listener, and is smart and intelligent.

The year 2020 is cited as a pivotal year for democracy in the United States, not only for the presidential election, but also congressional, state, and local elections. The 2016 election to the U. S. Presidency of an openly racist, mean-spirited man who hates and fears women sent a chill through the hearts of millions of women. His election prompted world-wide protests and sent 27,000 Sacramento women into the streets in January of 2017 for the first Women's March. His election also spurred thousands of women to mobilize and run for office at all levels of government in 2018 and beyond.

The sole woman serving on the City Council in 2016, Angelique Ashby (District 1, 2010–present), delivered an impassioned speech at the 2017 Sacramento Women's March, quoted in part below:

Ladies, I have 4 takeaways for you today:

Number One—your voice matters.
Your opinions and ideas are valuable.
You are worth listening to.
Your input and creativity make a difference.
No matter where you came from, what experiences you have, where you have been or how you got here, your story is important.

Number Two—we need your strength.
A healthy community has balance.
That means men and women are equally valued.
You need only to be your own true authentic self.
Whomever you were designed to be is exactly what we need. You are you and we are better because you are here.

Number Three—you are valuable.
You are not second in line.
You are not less than, or up-and-coming.
You are here right now, standing in the full power of who you were meant to be.

Number Four—you are not alone.
We stand with you.
We walk alongside you.
We lift each other up.
We are in this life together; you are supported.

Ladies, there is no singular person, nor administration, that can change these facts.
They can challenge us, but they will not prevail.
Because rising to our full potential is our destiny; it is not a variable ending.
The final chapter is already written and in it we are equal.
It is our responsibility:
To march
To lead
To educate
To drive
To persist
To endure

To keep going until we reach the mark
Look around you–this is our army–our weapons are education, law, experience, talent, and an unrelenting spirit driving us towards equality.
One: you matter
Two: you are strong
Three: you are valued
Four: you are not alone
So rise up and keep going...
We will do this together–because we were made for this moment–right now.

The Next Chapter

So, what's next for Sacramento? Which women will step up and take their rightful seats on the city councils, board of supervisors, and other elected and appointed boards in the region?

—Former Sacramento Mayor Heather Fargo

While this is physically the last chapter in the book, it is also the next chapter for women serving on appointed and elected boards in the county of Sacramento.

Hopefully, the history of the women who ran and served is interesting and educational. It should also be inspirational. More women are needed to run and serve. Delaine Eastin, the first, and so far only, woman ever elected to serve as the California Superintendent of Public Instruction (1995-2003), often states that, "When women represent 30% of an elected body, the conversation and priorities change." More focus is given to children, seniors, and people in need. Education, recreation, health, and other services that improve the quality of life, and in fact the very lives of people, become priorities. Libraries and community centers may see their hours extended and recreation and youth enrichments services may grow. The response to issues like truancy, code enforcement, the homeless, and civil rights, becomes more creative, and some would say, more effective.

Fortunately, many organizations have been formed to encourage, train, and elect women. Others encourage future candidates to prepare for elections by serving on local boards and commissions and leading community organizations. In this chapter we will identify these current organizations and the actual opportunities they present for women to consider.

In addition to the County Board of Supervisors, which has five members, there are other county-wide positions that are elected:

1. assessor
2. district attorney
3. sheriff
4. judges

There are now seven cities in the county that each have an elected city council, and many boards and commissions seeking volunteers. The county and most of the cities have never had a female majority, although most have had female mayors.

This book would not be complete without recognizing the many elected women outside of the city and county of Sacramento who were trailblazers in their communities.

Folsom incorporated in 1946 and was chartered as a city in 1990. Kerri Howell was first elected to the city council in 1998 and served as mayor in 2012 and 2014. Sarah Aquino was elected to the city council in 2018 and is serving as mayor in 2020.

Isleton incorporated in 1923
Pamela Bulahan currently serves as vice-mayor; Iva Walton is also on the council.

Galt incorporated in 1946
Four women have served as mayor in Galt: Marian O. Lawrence in 1982; Christina De La Cruz in 1996; Barbara Payne in 2008; and Marylou Powers in 2012 and 2016. Paige Lampson was elected to the council in 2018.

Rancho Cordova was incorporated in 2003
Linda Budge was elected to the original city council and is still serving in 2020. She is the first woman ever elected to the Rancho Cordova city council. She also served many years on the incorporation committee.

She served as the first mayor in 2004, then served again in 2008, 2013, and 2018. In November of 2020, Suri Pulipati, an engineer at Intel, became the first woman of color to win a seat on the council.

Citrus Heights was incorporated in 1997
Roberta MacGlashan was elected to the original Citrus Heights City Council in 1996. She served two terms, including two one-year terms as mayor in 1999 and 2002. Jeannie Bruins was elected to the Citrus Heights city council in 2002 and served as mayor in 2008, 2011, 2016, and 2019. Porsche Middleton was elected in 2018 as the third councilwoman and first African American woman to serve on the Citrus Heights city council.

Elk Grove was incorporated in 2000
Sophia Scherman was the first woman elected to the new city council in 2000 and served as mayor in 2010. The second woman, and first Asian American woman, elected to the city council was Stephanie Nguyen in 2018; and in 2020, Bobbi Singh-Allen became that city's first woman of color to win election as mayor.

Helpful Organizations
Organizations come and go, but as of this writing in 2021, the following organizations focus on electing women:

+ The Capital Women's Campaign, led by former Mayor Heather Fargo, was formed in early 2020 to bring Sacramento regional women's organizations together into a coalition committed to flexing their financial and political power, and to encourage women to engage in the political process.

+ The Sacramento Women & Girls Advancement Coalition brings together women who are focused on priorities that promote and assure gender equity in the city of Sacramento.

+ The National Women's Political Caucus (NWPC), founded in 1971, operates at the national, state, and local level to "identify, recruit, train, endorse and support women seeking public office." Their stated goal is to "increase the number of women in all aspects of political life." The Sacramento chapter of the NWPC is now chaired by former Sacramento City Councilmember Lauren Hammond, who is working to reinvigorate and grow the organization.

+ The Women Democrats of Sacramento County is believed to be the oldest continuously serving political club in California. The group supports Democratic candidates in the local area.

+ Emerge California was founded in 2003 to inspire women to run for office and hone their skills to win. They offer a five-month, 70-hour training program for Democratic women who are considering a run for elective office. (Based in Bay Area)

+ Close the Gap California leads a statewide campaign to achieve gender balance in the California Legislature. They recruit progressive, pro-choice, and pro-public school funding candidates, and support paths out of poverty. They are a great on-line resource for candidates. (Based in the Bay Area)

+ California Women Lead transformed from California Elected Women's Association for Education & Research in 2007 to make training and other support tools available for women who seek appointments at the state and local level and pursue appointments that reflect the diversity of California. (Based in Sacramento).

The county clerk and city clerks of each city maintain lists of positions and schedules of elections, and are the local experts on campaigns, voting, and elections. They also keep track of the many appointed positions in each jurisdiction. Serving in appointed positions is a way to prepare for elected office, by diving into the nitty-gritty of a board's duties, interacting with the public, and networking with others in the community.

In addition to those discussed already, here are more opportunities to serve your community:

1. Community Service Districts
2. Fire Districts
3. Flood Control Districts
4. Sacramento Municipal Utility District
5. Recreation and Park Districts
6. Resource Conservation Districts
7. Sacramento Office of Education
8. School Districts
9. Water and Irrigation Districts

For information on all elected positions in the county, consult Sacramento County Voter Registration and Elections at 916-875-6276. https://elections.saccounty.net

Refer to Voter Registration and Elections Index of Elected Officials

Congresswoman Doris Matsui

While the focus of *We Can Do This!* has been on women's contributions at the local government level, deep admiration and gratitude go to Congresswoman Doris Matsui, who became a trailblazer when she set aside her grief and found the courage to run for Congress following the death her husband, Congressman Bob Matsui, in 2005. She has served the 5th Congressional District with compassion and distinction for 16 years and she has risen to prominence as an effective congressional leader.

Like many women in this book, prior to her election to national office, Doris Matsui contributed her time and expertise to arts organizations in Sacramento, including the Crocker Art Museum, Sacramento Symphony, and public television station KVIE. Her support of the arts at the national level includes service on the Board of Regents for the Smithsonian Institution, the Council of the National Museum of African American History and Culture, and the National Symphony Board.

Her unique perspective as a survivor of a World War II Japanese American internment camp in Arizona, where she was born, has informed her work in the House of Representatives, especially after witnessing the divisive and racially motivated remarks and actions of former President Donald Trump targeting Muslims and Hispanics.

Matsui's untiring service to the Sacramento region has brought us greater flood protections, improved health care, more environment protection, advancements in clean energy, internet and technology policies that emphasize net neutrality, and more clean-tech jobs for our region. Her commitment to addressing climate change is unwavering, and she is an ardent supporter of educating girls and women in science, technology, engineering, and math (STEM). Her example is an inspiration for women considering how they might contribute to Sacramento's future as appointed and elected officials.

The next wave of political women will be standing on the shoulders of all of Sacramento's intrepid trailblazing political women.

BIBLIOGRAPHY

Interviews

Carlsen, Susan. Conducted by Christine Hunter, 6 Jan. 2020.

Collin, Illa and Knepprath, Kay. Conducted by Michele Drier, Christine Hunter, and Virginia Kidd. 14 Dec. 2017.

Fargo, Heather. Conducted by Christine Hunter and Virginia Kidd, 8 Jan. 2018.

Ferris, Lyla and Robie, Lynn. Conducted by Christine Hunter and Virginia Kidd, 21 March 2019.

Ferris, Lyla. Conducted by Christine Hunter. 1 May 2019.

Hagedorn, Jane. Conducted by Christine Hunter. 15 April 2014.

Hagedorn, Jane. Conducted by Christine Hunter. 3 Sept. 2019.

Hammond, Lauren. Conducted by Christine Hunter. 25 Nov. 2019.

Johnson, Muriel. Conducted by Christine Hunter, 3 Oct. 2019.

Johnson-Schulke, Collette. Conducted by Christine Hunter and Mary Ellen Shay, 20 Jul. 2019.

Knepprath, Kay. Conducted by Christine Hunter and Virginia Kidd, 11 Mar. 2019.

Knepprath, Kay. Conducted by Christine Hunter, 11 May 2019.

Mihanovich, Joyce. Conducted by Christine Hunter, 1 Apr. 2019.

Mihanovich, Joyce. Conducted by Christine Hunter, 15 Nov. 2019.

Mueller, Kim. Conducted by Christine Hunter and Virginia Kidd, 26 Apr. 2019.

O'Connor, Barbara. Conducted by Christine Hunter and Virginia Kidd, 26 Feb. 2016.

O'Connor, Barbara. Conducted by Christine Hunter and Virginia Kidd, 26 Apr. 2019.

Ortiz, Deborah. Conducted by Christine Hunter, 26 Sept. 2019.

Robie, Lynn and Mihanovich, Joyce. Conducted by Christine Hunter and Virginia Kidd, 21 Mar. 2019.

Rudin, Anne and Fargo, Heather. Conducted by Christine Hunter and Maryellen Burns, 17 Apr. 2014.

Saltzman, Estelle. Conducted by Michele Drier, Christine Hunter and Virginia Kidd, 26 Jul. 2019.

Sheedy, Sandra. Conducted by Christine Hunter and Collette Johnson-Schulke, 24 Jan. 2020.

Smoley, Sandra Conducted by Christine Hunter and Collette Johnson-Schulke, 17 Jan. 2020.

Works Cited

Barrow, Genoa. Former Sacramento City Councilmember Bonnie Pannell Passes. *Sacramento Observer*, 27 June 2017.

Beach, Cameron. A Success Story That Was Not Supposed to Happen. *Transportation Research Record 1361*, 1992.

Beach, Justin. *Women's Rights in the 1950s*, www.classroom.synonym.com, 25 June 2018.

Bizjak, Tony. Vintage Train Depot Set to Rise Again as Part of Dynamic City Hub. *The Sacramento Bee*, 15 Feb. 2015, p. A1.

Bramson, George. Letters to the Editor. *The Sacramento Bee*, 24 Mar. 2001.

Chandler, Jo. O'Connor. *Sacramento Magazine*, 2 Nov. 2006.

City Council Choices: Bradley and Robie. *The Sacramento Bee*, 24 Mar. 2001.

Council Saves Bacon of Family's Pet Pig. *The Sacramento Bee*, 15 Aug. 1991.

Dávila, Robert D. After Five Years, Domestic Partners Law Still Praised. *The Sacramento Bee*, 9 Nov. 1997, p. B1.

Dávila, Robert D. *The Sacramento Bee*, 29 Jan. 2006.

Driesbach, Willoughby and Moore. *Material Witness: Masters from California Crafts*, Sacramento, CA: Crocker Art Museum, 1999.

Fargo, Heather. [Guest]. *Studio Sacramento*. Interview by Scott Syphax. Public Television, KVIE. 20 Sept. 2019.

Fargo Seeks Unity on Depot—Transit Officials, Preservationists Duel over Railyard. *The Sacramento Bee*, March 2001, p. B1.

Future Face of Capital Politics: New City Council Could Have Four Women, Slow-Growth Force. *The Sacramento Bee*, 24 Sept. 1987, p. A1.

Gunsky, Fred. *Effie Yeaw—Teacher, Naturalist, Visionary*, Sacramento County Historical Society in cooperation with the American River Natural History Association, 1990.

Hauser, Susan. The Women's Movement in the '70s. Today: You've Come a Long Way, But... *Workforce*. 15 May 2012. workforce.com/article-author/susan-hauser.

Hayes, Peter J. *The Lower American River—Prehistory to Parkway*, The American River Natural History Association, 1977.

Heidorn, Nicolas. *Luella Johnston—California's First Councilwoman*, I Street Press, 2018.

Helgesen, Sally. *The Female Advantage—Women's Ways of Leadership*, Doubleday,1990.

Howard, John. Watch Your Language: City Seeks Neuter Form for Manhole. Associated Press, 8 May 1990, apnews.com/3962c20a9b644607b5d59aba2907f1.

Ihnat, Gwen. Whatever Happened to Home-economics Class? *The Takeout*, 15 June 2018. thetakeout.com/what-ever-happened-to-home economics-class-1826865440.

Knepprath, Kay. Stop at the Depot. *Opinions: Sacramento News and Review*, 12 April 2001, newsreview.com/sacramento/stop-at-the-depot/content?oid=5461.

League of Women Voters. About Us. www.lwv.org/About-us.

League of Women Voters of Sacramento County. my.lwv.org/california/sacramento-county, 4 Sep. 2019.

Lindelof, Bill. Partners Rule Kicks in Today—Unwed Pairs to Make it Legal. *The Sacramento Bee*, 16 Nov. 1992, p. B1.

---. Supervisor Looks Back—After 28 Years, Illa Collin is Stepping Down, Having Survived a Submarine and Donkey Basketball. *The Sacramento Bee*, 28 Dec. 2006.

Madoshi, Diana. [Guest]. *Studio Sacramento*. Interview by Scott Syphax. Public Television, KVIE, 20 Sept. 2019.

McLaughlin, Katie. "Five Things Women Couldn't Do in the 1960s. *CNN*, 25 Aug. 2014. https://www.cnn.com/2014/08/07/living/sixties-women-5-things

New Council Alignment Expected to Slow Growth. *The Sacramento Bee*, 5 Nov. 1987, p. B3.

Olson, Alexandra. Associated Press, *The Sacramento Bee*, 23 Dec. 2019.

Pajer, Nicole. Next Chapter. *Spry Living*, August 2019, pp.9-11.

Panneton, Judie. Queen Anne, Sacramento's Anne Rudin ambitiously embraces retirement. *The Sacramento Bee, Discover Sacramento*, 1999.

Pleading for Pet Pig—City Says Porky Has to Go, But Family's Fighting Back. *The Sacramento Bee*, 10 March 1991.

Public to Get a Glimpse of the Downtown Train Depot's Back Rooms. *The Sacramento Bee*, 22 Feb. 2017.

Questionnaires 1960. *United States Census Bureau*. https://www.census.gov/history/www/through_the_decades/questionnaires/1960_1.html

Questionnaires 1970. *United States Census Bureau*, https://www.census.gov/history/www/through_the_decades/questionnaires/1970_1.html

Rudin, Anne. Mayor Anne Rudin Speaks about Civil Unions. *Legends of Courage*. YouTube, 6 Feb. 2015.

Rules Aid Old Sac Horses. *The Sacramento Bee*, 14 August 1991, Metro, p. B3.

Shaw, Jeanie; Douglas, Eric; Tretheway, Ray. Celebrating 25 Years, *Sacramento Tree Foundation*, 2008, sactree.com/assets/files/STF_25YrHistoryFINAL.

Stodhill and Bower. Sacramento Most Diverse City, *Time Magazine*, 25 Aug. 2002, content.time/matopmartoc;e0.8599/340094,00. html.

Swatt, Steve; Swatt, Susie; LaVally, Rebecca; Raimundo, Jeff. *Paving the Way—Women's Struggle for Political Equality in California*, Berkeley Public Policy Press, Institute of Governmental Studies, University of California, Berkeley, 2019

The Millionth Tree—An Ambitious Dream Takes Root. Editorial. *The Sacramento Bee*, 1 May 2001, p. B6.

Time to Talk Trains: Sacramento Needs to End the Depot Debate. Editorial. *The Sacramento Bee*, 1 Apr. 2004, p. B6.

Yannello, Amy. Exit Outlook. *Sacramento News and Review*, 11 January 2007

INDEX OF NAMES